asian accents

asian accents

STUNNING DECORATING AND ENTERTAINING IDEAS

by Lisa Kim-Tribolati and Martyne Kupciunas
photos by Peter Mealin

PERIPLUS

contents

authors' preface 9 **a style both old and new**

introduction 10 **entertaining today**

the houses . **the food**

in living color 16 **mediterranean pleasures**

form & feng shui 24 **fragrant rice and rolls**

the comfort zone 36 **pacific rim cuisine**

pretty in pink 46 **high tea**

a touch of zen 54 **asian appetizers**

the pool house 64 **sushi and cocktails**

java style 74 **an indonesian buffet**

asian accents 84 **curried flavors**

ethnic chic 92 **cajun to asian**

a moonlit courtyard 100 **twilight supper**

indigo night 112 **fabulous finger food**

appendix 122 **tips, conversion table and index**

Published by Periplus Editions (HK) Ltd.,
with editorial offices at 130 Joo Seng Road,
#06-01/03, Singapore 368357 and 153 Milk Street,
Boston, MA 02109

Copyright © 2004 Periplus Editions (HK) Ltd.
All rights reserved.

ISBN 0-7946-0274-6
LCC Number 98-862 18

Printed in Singapore.

Acknowledgments:
Thanks to Tom Kupciunas, who continues to amaze me with his patience and understanding. M. K.
To John, Hong, Flora, and Susan. L. K.

Special thanks to Peter Mealin, for magically capturing our ideas and words in his photography, and for his and Choai Leng's patience, faith, and friendship. Thanks to Loretta Reilly, for her imagination and creativity; to Melanie Raymond, the best editor and friend with whom we were blessed; to Eric Oey, for his guidance and wisdom; and to Christina Ong, for her exceptional vision and unflappable support.

Many thanks to old and new friends who let us into their homes, shared ideas and recipes, and really made this book possible: Lucena Austria; Lucia Boey; Chan Soo Khian and SCDA Architects; David Droga; Carol Dunning; Stephen Falatko; Mary and Robert Franklin; Franz Friedl; Gan Jai Hong; Gan San San and Jacinta Gomes; Geh Min and Tong Ming Chuan; Terry and Robert Gibralter; Lyn and Mike Hall; Richard Helfer; Lincoln and Muffin Hoffman; Sandra Jarvis; Amy Katoh; Elizabeth and Chris Lin; Mark and Jamie Loveland; Burke and Cary McKinney; Philip Norfleet; Louis Phun and Colonial Home; Mrs Ong; Diana and T. K. Quek and Quek Associates; Emi Querubin; Magdeline Shaw; Leonie and Jean-Marie Simart; and Thomas Winslade.

Distributors:
Japan: Tuttle Publishing, Yaekari Building, 3F,
5-4-12 Osaki, Shinagawa-ku, Tokyo 141-0032.
Tel (03) 5437 017; Fax (03) 5437 0755
Email: tuttle-sales@gol.com

Asia Pacific: Berkeley Books Pte. Ltd.,
130 Joo Seng Road, #06-01/03, Singapore 368357.
Tel: (65) 6280 1330; Fax: (65) 6280 6290
Email: inquiries@periplus.com.sg

North America, Latin America & Europe:
Tuttle Publishing, 364 Innovation Drive,
North Clarendon, VT 05759-9436.
Tel: (802) 773 8930; Fax: (802) 773 6993
Email: info@tuttlepublishing.com

authors' preface

A style *both old and* new

left *This stately home is a classic example of a shophouse or terrace house interior in Singapore. The ornate furniture and half-doors are typically Peranakan.*

Pink, jade, turquoise and lemon: the elegant facades of terraced houses shimmer in the heat of the afternoon sun. Louvered wooden shutters are tightly shut against the glare while on the ground floors, the ornate *pintu pagars*, or half doors, guard the privacy of the occupants while allowing tropical breezes to enter. Welcome to Emerald Hill Road, Singapore.

When we moved to Singapore we were both lucky enough to find ourselves living in the renovated shophouses that fringe this colorful road. Shophouses are a traditional form of terraced house built early this century in the Malay Peninsula by the Peranakan communities (descendants of the Chinese traders who married Malay women). The interior spaces of these historic homes are long and narrow; on average, shophouses are just 18 feet wide. The open or enclosed central courtyards let in light and are perfect for the more casual style of entertaining encouraged by the equatorial heat.

This relaxed, leisurely style of entertaining exemplifies what we have come to think of as "the new Asian style", and inspired us to write this book. In the modern Asian home, the traditional furnishings and flavors of the Orient are infused with a Western sense of freedom and whimsy. In the realms of both food and decor, tradition has been spiced up with humor and a knack for the creative combination has replaced the formal. Inexpensive paper Chinese lanterns are coupled with rare and exquisite porcelain, and an airy lychee mousse might follow a piquant Cajun gumbo; all served on a fresh banana leaf. In today's international kitchen, cilantro and ginger are as much a necessity as olive oil and garlic.

Above all, the essence of this new style of decor and entertaining is a sense of balance and serenity; modernity is now at ease with tradition. This tranquility is also at the heart of life on Emerald Hill Road. Walking down this street you can imagine what life was like when this area was a nutmeg plantation. Children still play on the street and at night, the scents of different cuisines linger in the jasmine trees. Dainty bats dance in the light of the five-foot walkways. As for the cats of Emerald Hill Road . . . they are a book on their own.

introduction

Entertaining today

"Have you eaten today?" is a heartfelt Asian greeting, reflecting the importance of food not only as fuel for the body but for the well-being of the soul. In cities such as Singapore, Hong Kong and Bangkok, eating is a 24-hour pastime indulging all the senses, from the pungent aroma of fresh *chai* (tea) and breakfast noodles at daybreak, to the sound of fragrant *laksa* (seafood soup) being enthusiastically slurped at alfresco hawker stalls in the wee hours of the morning.

To dine together as family, friends or business colleagues is to establish and strengthen bonds—rarely is a business deal struck without feasting. As in the West, most socializing is done in restaurants and hotels, so an invitation to someone's home is an honor—just as it is an honor to host such a special occasion. Equal attention is lavished on presentation and preparation; both of the food itself and of the surroundings, so that they enhance the overall dining experience.

the occasion

There seems to be a festival on any given day of the year in Asia, where excuses to celebrate are as plentiful as lotuses in a temple pond. Look beyond Thanksgiving and Christmas and celebrate Chinese New Year, a Thai water festival, or a Balinese temple festival. Or relish the harvest seasons by welcoming the blossoming of spring flowers or the arrival of the first tender stalks of asparagus or succulent strawberries to the stores.

Whether the meal will be formal or informal, sit-down or buffet-style, a multi-course feast or a cocktail party, will be determined by the size of your guest list.

the decor

The aesthetics of your surroundings are determined more by your imagination and time than budget. If you are traveling in Asia, immerse yourself in specialty shops bursting with bargain baskets, fabrics for tablecloths, curios and conversational pieces. Closer to home, stroll through your neighborhood Chinatown and other ethnic shops in your area for interesting and inexpensive crockery, containers and objects to add a distinctive touch to your table and home. Or find new uses for treasures you already possess. In one

entertaining today

of the homes we visit, an old Japanese keyaki wood warehouse door is resurrected as an eye-catching tabletop. Silken cushions in saturated shades add exuberance to outdoor furnishings. The following pages will show you a multitude of uses for utensils and accessories from Indonesia, Japan, China and India, from wine coolers and ice buckets to floral containers and candleholders.

Concentrate on the rooms your guests will occupy, including the bathroom. Scented candles, a small flower or potpourri arrangement—perhaps in an incense holder or basket—and hand towels placed in a rustic wooden bowl exude atmosphere and luxury.

flower power

From religious offerings to personal adornment, tropical flowers are intrinsic to the Asian lifestyle. Available in abundance in their native habitats, they may be sourced inexpensively in the West from wholesale florists or Asian grocers. Exotic varieties such as the Bird of Paradise are striking sculptures in their own right; a single Casa Blanca lily makes a strong statement on an elegant table. A few stems of night-blooming jasmine or frangipani cast a net of intoxicating fragrance over an entrance hall or courtyard. In the West, the flowers usually take precedence over the container but in Asia, containers evoke fascinating vignettes of their own. White orchids spill like rice grains from an antique Thai basket; a Cambodian silver box cradles a treasure of roses and silver beads. Flowers often unfurl overnight so can be arranged the day before your occasion.

mood lighting

Asian evenings are suffused with the pungent aroma of incense and the heady scent of votive candles. Naked torches flare along balmy beachside walkways; a red paper lantern glows surreally in an inner-city temple entrance. Recreate the magic and theatre of the Orient in your home by placing candles in a betel-nut box or translucent fish lanterns in a kaleidoscope of rainbow hues. Be careful not to set scented candles too close to food as they may overpower its natural aroma.

left *Chill your best champagne in large terracotta bowls filled with ice.*
top *Hand towels are placed in a wooden bowl for the bathroom.*
above *An attractive arrangement of fresh fruit provides a thoughtful and welcoming touch for a guest's bedroom.*

introduction

right *Relaxing after a big occasion; a restorative cup of ginger tea is served with steamed buns (pau): Asian comfort food.*

the menu

Integral to any Asian-inspired occasion, the food you compose is the high note in your symphony of the senses. Check whether any of your guests have special dietary requirements for religious or health reasons and plan your menu accordingly. Choose the main course first, then the starter and dessert, balancing flavor, texture and color. If possible, select dishes which can be prepared in advance and served cold or at room temperature to avoid having to cook right before serving. You may want to purchase a dessert to save time; a Chinese or Vietnamese bakery offers enticing alternatives to their Western counterparts. This will free you to relax and savor your guests' delighted pleas for an encore.

serving style

These days, just about any serving style is acceptable, as long as it is suited to the food, seating arrangement and number of guests. Substitute antique chopsticks for knives and forks if appropriate. Whether food is served Japanese-style on individual plates or Chinese-style on platters, effective juxtapositions of color and texture can be attained if you follow the professional chefs' practice of sketching the arrangement.

Because of the casual nature of much modern entertaining, particularly in the sultry tropics, finger foods wrapped in fresh herbs and vegetables are emphasized in this book. Serving dishes should complement your appetizing morsels, tempting guests to feast first with their eyes. Long before designer products caught on, traditional Japanese crockery unveiled the importance of packaging. Experiment with these exquisitely versatile vessels, or opt for the natural containers used in some of our recipes, in which salmon tartare nestles on glistening shiso leaves and sorbet brims from frozen mangosteen cups.

having fun

Planning is the key to successful entertaining. With the tips and ideas gleaned from this book and a dash of organization (lists are a good idea), your passage to the East promises to be a sublime sensation for all concerned. Entertaining should above all be fun; we wish you a delightful and memorable time.

in living color

mediterranean pleasures

in living color

Fashionable lemon-lime and turquoise hues streak happily across this living room. Inspired by the saturated colors of the tropics, the vibrant and sophisticated fabrics used here add zest and excitement to their surroundings.

If you have always opted for a beige and cream color scheme and are a little hesitant about introducing strong, bold colors, start with patterned pillows, cushion covers or a tablecloth. Paint a guest bathroom in dazzling colors or drape a bright scarf over your favorite chair. Try personalizing your own linen. We stenciled gold geckos on white and gold-trimmed linen napkins. They add an element of surprise to a table setting and are an amusing and creative alternative to plain napkins.

With all this vivid color to occupy the eye, decorations are kept to a minimum. Large tropical flower arrangements provide all the interest here; not only are they colorful, but their unusual shapes and sizes add drama to a room. A single, well-placed flower or leaf may be all you need to accent a corner. Here we've displayed heliconia in a large glass vase; a graceful Mokoyama leaf is used to hide the stems.

This relaxed Mediterranean-style lunch for family or friends was inspired by the color scheme. Glossy red and yellow bell peppers filled with caponata are served on a cobalt blue dish. The dishes here can all be prepared the night before and served at room temperature, which makes them wonderfully versatile.

far left *Sunflowers add a dash of color to a platter of beef tenderloin. Think about shape as well as color when choosing flowers, the gold and yellow tones of these sunflowers and tulips may be similar but the different shapes provide contrast.*
left *The simplicity of a glass vase works best for some floral arrangements. To prevent water from getting cloudy, add one teaspoon of liquid bleach per quart of water.*
below *Fresh fruit, as appealing to look at as to eat, is the main ingredient of dessert. The whimsical gecko napkins featured here were stenciled especially for this lunch. See page 122 to find out how to stencil your favorite design on your own napkins.*

in living color . mediterranean pleasures

A Sunday lunch featuring Mediterranean-influenced foods that are bold, fresh and flavorful seems to fit nicely with the spirit of the room. A roasted beef tenderloin is marinated with robust Mediterranean and Asian spices and accompanied by caponata served in orange and red bell peppers. To finish the meal, an array of sweet berries and tropical fruit is served with a ginger-orange cream; a great finish to a midday meal so light the post-lunch siesta is optional.

beef tenderloin

ingredients
1/2 cup whole black peppercorns
1 (5-pound) tenderloin fillet

marinade
1 tablespoon tomato paste
1/2 teaspoon ground cardamom
1 teaspoon ground paprika
2 cloves garlic, chopped finely
1 cup soy sauce
3/4 cup red wine vinegar
1 cup water

Press peppercorns into beef and place in 9 x 13-inch baking dish. Mix all marinade ingredients together until well combined. Pour marinade over beef, cover and refrigerate for 6 hours, turning the beef over once after 3 hours to marinate both sides evenly.

Preheat oven to 350 ° F when ready to roast. Drain marinade from baking dish, cover beef with foil and roast for 40–45 minutes. Allow beef to sit for 10 minutes before carving to allow the juices to settle.

Serves 10.

note: *Reduce cooking time for rare meat.*

caponata

ingredients
12 cups eggplant, cut into 1/2-inch-square cubes
(3 medium eggplant)
1 tablespoon salt
1/2 cup extra virgin olive oil
2/3 cup finely chopped onion
1 cup finely chopped celery
2 large bell peppers (yellow if available), chopped
8 ounces black Calamata olives, pitted and chopped
1 cup fresh tomato sauce
2 tablespoons capers
3 tablespoons balsamic vinegar
Salt and pepper to taste
12 red and yellow bell peppers for serving containers

Sprinkle the eggplant with salt and set aside in a colander to drain. After 30 minutes, pat dry and set aside.

Heat 1/4 cup of the olive oil in a skillet and add onion, celery and chopped bell peppers. Cook over moderate heat stirring frequently, until onions are translucent and peppers slightly browned, about 5 minutes. Transfer to a bowl with a slotted spoon.

Divide eggplant into 3 batches. Pour 2 tablespoons of oil into the skillet and sauté the first batch, stirring constantly until soft and lightly browned, 5–8 minutes. Transfer to a large bowl and continue with the remaining 2 batches of eggplant, using the remaining olive oil.

Add onion, pepper and celery mixture, olives, tomato sauce, balsamic vinegar, and capers to cooked eggplant and mix. Drain any excess liquid. Add salt and pepper to taste. Can be served warm or at room temperature.

Serves 10–12.

presentation: *Serve caponata in whole bell peppers as shown here. Cut the tops off yellow and red bell peppers and remove the ribs and seeds. Slightly trim the bases so peppers stand flat. Fill with caponata and cover with "lid." Arrange and serve on a platter.*

Caponata.

fruit salad with ginger & orange cream

ingredients

1 (8- ounce) container mascarpone cheese
1/3 cup sour cream
2 tablespoons brown sugar
2 teaspoons grated orange zest
1/2 teaspoon grated fresh ginger
6 cups of assorted fresh fruit: strawberries, pears, apple, kiwi fruit, starfruit, and red or green seedless grapes

Stir together cheese, sour cream, brown sugar, orange zest and fresh ginger. Cover and chill for up to 24 hours.

Peel, seed and slice all the fruit except for the strawberries and grapes, which can be left whole. Arrange decoratively on a platter and serve with the ginger and orange cream. Serves 8.

presentation: *An alternative presentation to the one above is to make a fruit salad with oranges, strawberries, kiwi fruit and mango and divide into large wine glasses, making sure you also include any juices from the fruit. Spoon the ginger and orange cream into a pastry bag with a large nozzle and pipe some onto the fruit in a decorative way. Garnish with mint leaves.*

form & feng shui

fragrant rice & rolls

form & feng shui

left *A cantilevered staircase, magically suspended in the air like a huge sculpture, descends to the ground floor.*

This elegant home is a play on form, function and *feng shui*. *Feng shui*, the ancient Chinese art of placement, holds that the proper placement of furniture and objects will greatly enhance the flow of *chí i*, or energy, and bring prosperity to the prudent occupants of the *feng shui* building.

Everything in this architect's home flows in perfect harmony. The monochromatic color scheme was chosen to expand the long narrow space imposed by the structure of the shophouse. This subdued background also serves to highlight the Southeast Asian paintings hanging on the wall. In fact, the house was built to showcase the family's much-prized collection of Asian art, which includes rare and exquisite sculptures as well as paintings. It is obvious that careful attention was paid to the positioning of each piece—whether in deference to the art of the geomancer or just the art itself. An otherwise stark wall on the first floor provides the perfect backdrop for the drama of the traditional Japanese wedding kimono. The elegance of its design and the subtlety of the fabric's colors and textures are just some of the aspects of its beauty.

"Good fortune" is the theme of the dining room featured on page 31, hence red, considered an auspicious color in Chinese culture, is the keynote color of the decor. The shapes and colors used in the lantern festival painting are echoed in this table setting for a formal lunch. Traditional Chinese plates decorated with dragon motifs symbolizing prosperity are placed on the red paper fans which are an exotic alternative to placemats. Inlaid enamel chopsticks rest on pewter fish and the Winter Cherry flowers used as the floral centerpiece repeat the lantern shapes in the painting. Gold Chinese lunar calendar animals are scattered around the table for more good luck and to add a quirky and personal touch. In contrast to the refined opulence of the setting, lunch is classic Singaporean hawker stall food: Popiah (a version of fresh spring rolls), and the ubiquitous and much loved Hainanese Chicken Rice.

above *A rare Chinese stone frieze decorates a wall of the indoor pond. Koi, the good luck fish, play beneath the surface.*

right *This stunning glass dining table is a collector's item. An antique Chinese drum made of leather and brass fittings has been put to ingenious use to create the base of the table.*

previous pages *The beautifully designed staircase cuts a strong vertical swathe through the dining room. The functional elements of this home have been considered as carefully as the decorative ones.*

form & feng shui • fragrant rice and rolls

For lunch, dishes synonymous with Singapore were chosen: Popiah and Chicken Rice. Popiah are the Singaporean version of fresh spring rolls and have been modified here so they can be served as a first course. In case the authentic wrappers are hard to find, we also used crepe wrappers, shaping them into small packets stuffed with the filling. Chicken Rice is simplicity itself, consisting only of poached chicken and aromatic rice flavored with chicken stock. Serve with chili sauce for an added punch of flavor. Following the main course, fresh fruit and nuts dipped in chocolate are served near the tranquil *koi* pond. If you prefer to continue with the Chinese menu, serve egg custard tarts bought from a Chinese bakery.

easy *popiah*

ingredients

filling

2 tablespoons vegetable oil
4 cloves garlic, minced
1 pound pork loin, cut into very thin strips
3 cups finely sliced jicama
1 cup finely sliced carrots
1 cup water
1 tablespoon oyster sauce

for wraps

60 (5 x 5-inch) frozen spring roll wrappers or
45 (8 x 8-inch) crepes
Hoisin sauce
1 1/2 cups bean sprouts
1 cup snow peas, blanched, refreshed, and finely chopped
3/4 pound small shrimp, cooked and chopped
1/2 pound Chinese sausage, steamed for 20 minutes, cooled, and thinly sliced

45 scallions, green part only, blanched and refreshed in ice water

Heat the vegetable oil in a skillet, add garlic and cook for 30 seconds, stirring constantly. Add pork and cook until no longer pink, about 3 to 5 minutes. Add jicama and carrots and cook for 5 minutes, stirring constantly.

Add water and oyster sauce and bring to a boil. Reduce heat and simmer uncovered for about 25 to 30 minutes, stirring occasionally, or until jicama and carrots are tender and most of the water has evaporated. The mixture should still be moist. When cooked, remove the vegetable-pork mixture from heat and let cool.

For the popiah wraps:
If using spring roll wrappers, defrost and keep covered with a damp tea towel to prevent wrappers from drying out. Take one wrapper and cut into 3 equal strips. Lay a wrapper on your work surface with one of the corners toward you. Place one strip across the center of the wrapper. (You will need 4 wrappers for every 3 rolls.) Spread 1/2 teaspoon of hoisin sauce on the center strip. Top with a tablespoon or so of the pork mixture. Then scatter some bean sprouts, snow peas, shrimp, and sausage over the filling.

Fold the corner closest to you toward the far corner but stop about an inch short of the corner. Then fold the right corner over the center followed by the left, making sure they overlap. Take one scallion, gently wrap around the roll and tie to hold the roll together. Repeat with the remaining wrappers and ingredients. Keep the finished popiah covered with a damp tea towel until ready to serve.

If using frozen crepes (as shown here), defrost, and using a 6-inch diameter pastry cutter, cut circles out of each crepe. Keep the crepes covered with damp tea towel to prevent them from drying out. Follow the instructions above, using 1 teaspoon of the hoisin sauce, 1 1/2 tablespoons of the filling and slightly more of the individual toppings. If using crepes, there is no need to add the extra strip as the crepes are already sufficiently thick.
Makes 45 popiah packets.

note: Pork-vegetable mixture can be made a day ahead and refrigerated. The other ingredients can also be prepared a day ahead and refrigerated. The rolls can be made an hour in advance but should be kept covered with a damp tea towel at room temperature.

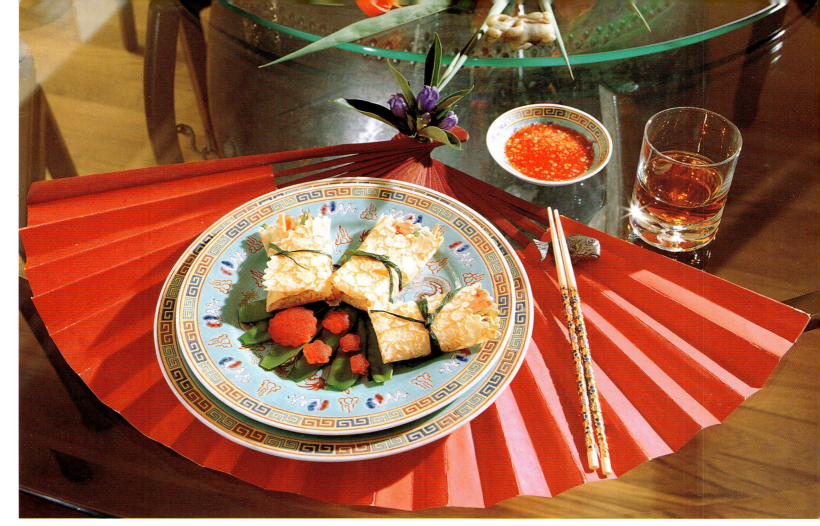

Easy Popiah.

chili sauce

ingredients

1/4 cup chopped red chili pepper (remove the seeds and inner membrane if you prefer a milder sauce)

4 cloves garlic, sliced

4 tablespoons rice vinegar

1 tablespoon sugar, or more to taste

Put all the ingredients into a blender and purée. Makes about 1/3 cup.

note: Chili sauce can be refrigerated in a glass jar for up to a week.

form & feng shui . **fragrant rice and rolls**

chicken rice

ingredients

chicken

6 chicken breasts on the bone, with skin
Salt
5 quarts water
1 (6-inch) piece ginger, cut into 1-inch thick slices and bruised with the side of the knife

rice

1 tablespoon sesame oil
2 cloves garlic, minced
1 tablespoon minced fresh ginger
3 cups long-grain rice, rinsed and drained
6 cups chicken stock from above
1/4 teaspoon salt

garnish

Cucumbers, tomatoes and cilantro (optional) for garnish

To cook the chicken:
Season the chicken breasts with salt and rub it in. Let sit for 15 to 30 minutes. Bring the water and ginger to a boil in a large stock pot. Add the chicken breasts and bring to a second boil. If the chicken is not entirely covered with liquid, add more water. Reduce heat to a simmer, cover and cook until chicken is done, about 20 minutes.

Remove the chicken from the pot. Reserve 6 cups of the cooking liquid for the rice. Skim the fat from the surface of the chicken stock and set aside. When ready to serve, debone the cooled chicken breasts and slice crosswise into smaller pieces.

For the rice:
Heat the sesame oil in a pot. Add garlic and ginger and sauté for 1 minute, taking care not to burn the garlic. Stir in the rice and sauté for 1 minute, constantly stirring so the rice is coated with the oil.

Add the chicken stock and bring to a boil. Cover pot, reduce heat to low and simmer until rice is tender and the liquid absorbed, about 20 minutes. Remove the pot from the heat and let stand for about 10 minutes without removing the cover.
Serves 6.

presentation: Pack rice firmly in a bowl, place a plate over the bowl and overturn the bowl onto the plate. Carefully remove the bowl to unmold the rice. Arrange the chicken slices around the side of the rice and garnish with sliced cucumber, tomato, and sprigs of cilantro. Serve with chili sauce (recipe page 33) and dark soy sauce in bowls on the side.

notes: The chicken can be cooked a day ahead. Refrigerate chicken and reserved stock to cook the rice. If you plan on cooking rice often, an electric automatic rice cooker is a must-have appliance; it cooks perfect rice every time. They are inexpensive and can be found at Asian markets.

Chicken Rice.

chocolate *dipped fruit*

ingredients

1/2 pound of good-quality dark or milk chocolate, chopped

Your choice of a variety of fruit, such as whole strawberries, slices of apple, pear, kiwi fruit, or banana

Your choice of whole shelled nuts, such as pistachios, macadamia, walnuts, hazelnuts, cashews or almonds

Place chopped chocolate in a heat-proof bowl and place over another bowl of hot water. Stir chocolate until melted.

Dip half the piece of fruit or fruit slice into the chocolate and swirl to cover. Place on baking sheets lined with parchment paper. Continue with remaining fruit. Refrigerate to set.

For the nuts:
Spread nuts out on baking sheet lined with parchment paper. Transfer chocolate into piping bag and pipe chocolate over an individual nut until covered. Continue with remaining nuts. Refrigerate to set.

note: *If chocolate begins to stiffen, place the bowl over hot water.*

the comfort zone

pacific rim cuisine

the comfort zone

As work encroaches ever further into our leisure time and technology changes the way that we do business, home has become an extension of the office for many people, if not the office itself.

Carved wooden doors from Thailand lead the way into this multifunctional home that allows the owner to host a dinner for clients as easily as relax in front of the television set with the family. While the first consideration for the design of this interior was comfort, the challenge was to maintain the intimacy of a family environment while recognizing the owner's desire to conduct business at home. The highback wing chairs, comfortable classic sofas and golf memorabilia are combined to create an atmosphere of ease and leisure, while the large dining-room table and boardroom-like chairs add a necessary touch of corporate formality. The television set and stereo are cleverly housed in an attractive cabinet, allowing the owner to shut them away when the living room is being used for business.

As a change of pace from the anonymity of conference rooms and restaurants, this business lunch was brought home. For this purpose, a table setting which is sophisticated and formal enough for clients was needed. Crisply pressed white linen placemats and napkins, white china, and gleaming silverware are *de rigueur* corporate dining style and are complemented here with an eye-catching arrangement of bright tropical flowers (following pages). For the lunch menu, the delights of Pacific Rim cuisine are offered. Foods from the New World blend with exotic Asian produce and are prepared in a simple but stylish manner to highlight the fresh natural flavors of the ingredients.

the comfort zone . pacific rim cuisine

Lunch starts with a rich, velvety pumpkin soup, served in a whole pumpkin shell for a stunning presentation. Smaller individual pumpkins can also be used the same way and make excellent individual soup bowls. For the main course, pan-fried pork chops are teamed with a zesty mango salsa; a simple dish of baby kai-lan is served on the side. Green tea ice cream, a modern Japanese classic, completes a meal that is impressive yet light enough to suit a working lunch. This menu is perfect if you have a tight schedule.

pumpkin soup

ingredients

1 whole (4-pound) pumpkin
2 tablespoons butter
1/2 cup diced onion
2 tablespoons diced shallots
1 teaspoon ground cumin
1 teaspoon brown sugar
3 cups chicken broth
Salt and ground black pepper to taste
1/2 cup cream

Cut the top off the pumpkin and set aside. Scoop out the seeds and discard. With a heavy spoon, scrape out the flesh from inside the pumpkin and the lid. You will have about $1^1/2$ pounds of flesh. Dice the flesh into 1 x $1^1/2$-inch cubes and set aside.

Heat butter in a saucepan and add onion and shallots and cook for about 3 minutes or until soft, stirring constantly. Add pumpkin flesh and cook over low heat for about 10 minutes stirring occasionally. Add cumin and sugar and cook for 2 minutes.

Add chicken broth and bring to a boil. Reduce heat to a simmer, cover and cook about 30 minutes or until pumpkin is soft, stirring occasionally.

Meanwhile, if you wish to to serve the soup in the pumpkin shell, wash and dry the inside and outside. Place the shell, with its lid on, in a 325 ° F oven for 15–20 minutes to warm for serving.

Purée the soup in a blender. Depending on the size of your blender, you may need to do this in two batches. Return soup to a clean saucepan and season to taste. Gently reheat soup and if too thick, thin with more broth. Stir in the cream, taking care not to let the soup boil.

To serve: ladle soup into the warmed pumpkin shell and bring to the table.
Serves 6.

presentation: *To add height and drama to a pumpkin, secure a pineapple top to the pumpkin lid as we have done here, using a pin. This will also facilitate lifting the lid.*

notes: *If you are pressed for time, serve the soup in soup bowls instead of the whole pumpkin. Carefully slice the pumpkin into quarters with a large, heavy knife. Remove the seeds and discard. Lay the quarter on its side and slice away the skin with the knife. Cut the flesh into cubes and proceed as above. Soup without the shell can be made two days ahead and refrigerated or frozen for up to a month.*

Pumpkin Soup.

steamed baby kai-lan

ingredients
24 stalks baby kai-lan, trimmed
2 tablespoons sesame oil
Salt and pepper

Steam *kai-lan* in steamer for 5–7 minutes and transfer to a bowl. Toss with sesame oil, and salt and pepper to taste.
Serves 6.

note: *Kai-lan is the Cantonese name of the green leafy vegetable otherwise known as Chinese broccoli or Chinese kale. Baby kai-lan is the miniature version. If preferred, or if kai-lan is not available, use spinach leaves.*

the comfort zone . pacific rim cuisine

pork loin with mango salsa & raspberry sauce

ingredients

mango salsa

1 firm, ripe mango, flesh cut into $1/4$-inch dice (about 1 cup)
1 ripe kiwi fruit, flesh cut into $1/4$-inch dice (about $1/4$ cup)
1 tablespoon finely chopped red onion
2 tablespoons mint leaves, chopped
1 tablespoon freshly squeezed lime juice

raspberry sauce

4 tablespoons raspberry preserves
$1/2$ cup red wine vinegar

6 boneless pork loin chops, each 1-inch thick
Salt and pepper
1 tablespoon butter

For the mango salsa: Mix all the salsa ingredients together in a bowl, cover with plastic wrap and set aside.

For the raspberry sauce: Whisk preserves and vinegar together in a saucepan and bring to a boil. Reduce heat and let simmer for about 10 minutes, or until sauce thickens. Remove from heat and keep warm. The sauce will continue to thicken as it cools.

For the pork loins: Season pork loins with salt and pepper. Melt butter in a hot skillet, add pork loins to the melted butter and cook for about 3 minutes on each side. Reduce to medium heat, cover skillet and cook the pork loins until done, approximately 5–7 minutes. Serves 6.

presentation: To serve, place a tablespoon or so of sauce onto each plate, top with pork loin, and some mango-kiwi salsa. Arrange the kai-lan leaves around the pork.

note: Boneless chicken breasts can be substituted for pork.

sautéed shiitake mushrooms

ingredients

3 tablespoons olive oil
$1^{1}/4$ pounds shiitake mushrooms, caps sliced and stems removed
2 cloves garlic, minced
6 tablespoons Madeira
Salt, to taste
3 tablespoons flat-leaf parsley, chopped

Heat one tablespoon of olive oil in a nonstick pan over high heat. Add a third of the mushrooms and sauté until mushrooms soften and begin to brown, approximately 2 to 3 minutes.
　　Add a third of the minced garlic and cook for 1 minute, stirring constantly to avoid burning the garlic.
　　Add 2 tablespoons of the Madeira and salt to taste. Cook until the Madeira has evaporated, about 1 minute. Transfer to bowl.
　　Repeat the above twice with the remaining ingredients.
　　Add parsley to the bowl of sautéed mushrooms and mix.
Serves 6.

Pork Loin with Mango Salsa & Raspberry Sauce.

green *tea ice* cream

ingredients
3 ounces green tea powder
1 cup cognac or brandy
10 cups fresh milk
2 cups fresh cream
2 2/3 cups instant nonfat milk powder
3 1/2 cups sugar

Put the green tea powder in a bowl, add the cognac and mix well to form a paste. Put the milk, cream, milk powder, and sugar into another bowl and mix well. Transfer the milk and cream mixture to a saucepan and bring to a boil over moderate heat. Remove from the heat and allow to cool to a lukewarm temperature, then add the green tea paste, mixing well.

    Chill immediately in the freezer until ice crystals start to form around the edges of the container. Put the mixture into a blender or food processor and blend for a few seconds to break up the crystals. Return to the freezer and leave until set. Alternatively, freeze in an ice cream maker according to the manufacturer's instructions.

Serves 8.

pretty in pink
high tea

47

pretty in pink

Afternoon tea is a rarity in today's busy world, a deliberate pause in the day for serenity and sustenance. It is a much-loved tradition that conjures romantic images of bygone days when tea and other luxuries from the Orient were traded in Europe and the New World. It is also one of the most enjoyable ways to entertain and unwind with friends and acquaintances.

Afternoon tea has never gone out of fashion at the grandest hotels, and with good reason. Its versatility allows you to adapt it to your needs: Plan a cozy and intimate gathering with good friends and lots of gossip; or present a lavish and opulent affair reminiscent of lazy afternoons and long white dresses.

Bring out your finest china and your best lace or linen tablecloth, and treat your guests to a variety of sweets and savories. Not owning a complete china or antique silver tea set should not stop you from hosting a high tea; mix and match with different pieces of china and silver found at flea markets or tag sales. The pretty buffet-style tea table here was created with touches from two great tea-drinking cultures: the English and the Chinese. Classic Wedgewood crockery and a grand silver tea service contrast with inexpensive Chinese napkin holders, and an antique Chinese screen depicting aristocratic ladies at a tea party affords an added note of gentility in the background.

Roses provide the perfect touch floral touch for your table; the soft charm of their pastel shades evocative of an English garden. This setting is as perfect a blend of East meets West as the tea that is being served, romantic unruffled elegance at its best.

pretty in pink • **high tea**

For afternoon tea, serve a generous selection of sweet and savory tidbits. Instead of the traditional cucumber sandwiches, we served spicy curry and hearty beef puffs, open tuna sandwiches, and salmon ribbons. Cater to the sweet tooths among your guests with scones and preserves, which can be bought from any of the good bakeries in your area. Consider setting out a selection of tea leaves, such as Darjeeling, English Breakfast or Lapsang Souchong, in bowls, each clearly labeled. You may even want to break from custom and provide some herbal teas such as camomile, lemon-balm or mint. Provide a couple of pots of hot water and sugar, honey, milk, cream, and lemon wedges.

vegetable curry puffs

ingredients

2 tablespoons vegetable oil
1 large onion, diced (or about 1 1/3 cups)
2 cloves garlic, minced
1 teaspoon minced fresh ginger
2 cups cooked potatoes, peeled and cut into small cubes
1/2 cup fresh or frozen green peas, thaw if frozen
1 teaspoon ground coriander
1/2 teaspoon ground cumin
1/4 teaspoon ground turmeric
1/4 teaspoon garam masala
1/4 teaspoon cayenne, or more to taste
1/2 teaspoon salt
2 teaspoons fresh lemon juice
5 (10 x 10-inch) frozen puff pastry sheets

Heat the oil in a large skillet. Add onion and cook until soft, about 3 minutes. Stir in garlic and ginger and continue stirring for approximately 1 minute or until aromatic.

Add the cooked potatoes and cook for 5 minutes, stirring occasionally.

Stir in peas, coriander, cumin, turmeric, *garam masala*, cayenne and salt. Mix until all ingredients are well incorporated. Don't worry if some of the potatoes get mashed in the mixing process. Cook for about a minute. Remove from heat and add the lemon juice. Let potato mixture cool completely.

Preheat oven to 400 ° F.

Cut pastry into 3-inch circles with a pastry cutter. Take one circle of pastry and place about a teaspoon or so of potato mixture in the center. Bring the sides of the circle together over the filling and pinch the edges tightly to form a half circle. Repeat with the remaining potato mixture and pastry circles.

Place curry puffs on a baking sheet and bake until puffed and golden brown, about 15 to 20 minutes.

Makes 40 small puffs.

colonial tuna sandwiches

ingredients

1 cup solid white tuna packed in water, well drained (four 6-ounce cans)
1 tablespoon minced shallot
Dash of ground paprika
1/3 cup mayonnaise
Mini pita bread, or toasted white bread cut into 3-inch rounds, or toasted baguette slices
Chutney
Parsley leaves to garnish

Combine tuna, shallot, and paprika. Mix in 1/3 cup mayonnaise and add more until the desired consistency is achieved. Spoon 1 tablespoon of tuna mixture onto each mini-pita, toasted white bread or baguette, and top with 1 teaspoon of chutney of your choice. Garnish with parsley leaf.

Makes approximately 20 sandwiches.

note: *The tuna mixture can be made up to 2 days in advance and stored in the refrigerator.*

Colonial Tuna Sandwiches.

smoked salmon ribbons

ingredients

ribbons
Cucumber
Smoked salmon, sliced thinly
Caper-cream cheese spread

caper-cream cheese spread
6 tablespoons cream cheese
1 tablespoon capers, drained and chopped
Makes about 6 tablespoons

Slice cucumber lengthwise into 20 thin slices with a mandoline or Japanese slicer. Trim the smoked salmon pieces to fit the cucumber slices.

Spread a cucumber slice with some caper-cream cheese spread and top with a slice of smoked salmon. Starting at one end, roll the cucumber and salmon slices and secure with a toothpick.

For the caper-cream cheese spread:
Mix cream cheese and capers together in a bowl. Refrigerate until ready to use.
Makes about 20 ribbons.

note: *The spread can be made a day ahead and kept in the refrigerator.*

spicy madeira beef puffs

ingredients

1 teaspoon vegetable oil
1 pound ground beef
1 tablespoon unsalted butter
1/2 large onion, finely diced
2 cloves garlic, minced
2 cups button mushrooms, thinly sliced
3 tablespoons Madeira
2 to 3 drops Tabasco, or more to taste
2 teaspoons Worcestershire sauce
1/4 teaspoon salt
Ground black pepper to taste
4 (10 x 10-inch) frozen puff pastry sheets,
or 5 (10 x 10-inch) frozen puff pastry sheets for smaller puffs

Heat the vegetable oil in a large skillet. Cook beef for about 5 minutes or until brown, stirring constantly to break up large bits. Remove beef from pan with a slotted spoon and set aside.

In another pan heat the butter and add the diced onion. Cook until soft, stirring constantly, this should take about 3 minutes. Add garlic and continue stirring for 1 minute, taking care not to burn the garlic.

Add the cooked beef, mushrooms, Madeira, Tabasco and Worcestershire sauce, salt and pepper, and cook until mushrooms turn soft and the liquid has evaporated, about 5 minutes. Remove from heat and let cool.

Preheat oven to 400 ° F.

Cut a pastry sheet into 4 squares. Take one square and place 3 tablespoons of beef filling in the center. Form a triangle by folding one corner over to meet the opposite corner, and then press the edges together tightly. Continue with remaining ingredients.

Place puffs on a baking sheet and bake until pastry is puffed and golden brown, about 20–25 minutes.

For smaller puffs:
Cut a pastry sheet into thirds vertically, then into thirds horizontally, creating 9 squares. Take one square and place 1 tablespoon of beef filling in the center and continue as described above until you have used up all the ingredients. Baking time for smaller puffs may need to be reduced to 15–20 minutes.
Makes 15 puffs or 40 small puffs.

notes: *It is easier to work with the puff pastry if it is partially thawed, as the dough can sometimes be too soft to work with when fully thawed. Just place the pastry back in the freezer for about 5 minutes to stiffen the dough. Both curry and beef puffs can be made well in advance and frozen; a terrific standby for when those unexpected guests visit or you have a spontaneous cocktail party. When ready to serve, place the puffs in the oven without defrosting and bake for 15-25 minutes, depending on the size of the puffs.*

Spicy Maderia Beef Puffs.

puff pastry canapés

ingredients

Frozen puff pastry sheets
Your preferred topping: crème fraîche, caviar, smoked salmon and capers, cheese spread, ice cream

Keep a supply of puff pastry in your freezer for last minute canapés. Take a $2^1/_2$-inch round cookie cutter and cut circles from a sheet of pastry. Place on a baking sheet and bake at 375 °F for 10-15 minutes or until the pastry is golden and puffed up. Remove from the oven and, with your thumb wrapped in a tea towel to prevent burning yourself, gently press down on the center of the each puff. Fill the puffs with your topping of desire—crème fraîche and caviar, smoked salmon and capers; pipe in your favorite cheese spread; or for sweets, place a small scoop of ice cream in the center and cover with your favorite topping.

a touch of zen

asian appetizers

a touch of zen

left *A living space of warmth and serenity: balance and restraint are the key elements of the design philosophy in this home.*
next page *Sunlight casts a warm glow over the enclosed courtyard and indoor bamboo garden.*

Inspired by the simplicity of Zen, this home is an example of uncluttered elegance. Simplicity of form, strong lines and bold compositions combine to form an interior that is balanced in shape as well as color and texture. Sculptured pieces of furniture and unique artifacts have been harmoniously arranged to utilize the narrow space in this Peranakan shophouse.

The subtlety of the decor and the clean lines of the furniture create an atmosphere of serenity, providing the perfect background for the rare and exquisite objects that have been lovingly collected from many parts of Asia—Burma, China, Indonesia and Japan, to name a few. Every object is a testament of the owners' longstanding fascination with the East and has its own anecdote, to be shared with visitors. The trunk of a large teak tree from Sulawesi, crafted into a coffee table, is nicknamed "King Kong" because it takes four people to lift it. Behind the table, three Japanese washi paper lamps rise up from the floor like illuminated sails, their delicacy emphasized by the rugged and earthbound qualities of the table. Although simple, this room is far from stark. The restrained decorating style enhances the beauty of the furniture and *objéts-d'arts*, which complement rather than compete with each other. If the furnishings in this interior are important, so too the spaces between them.

To create this relaxed and informal atmosphere for an evening of casual drinks with close friends, we lit candles nestled in a betel-nut box. A length of fabric from East Bali is draped over the table which has served as the focal point for many happy, impromptu social gatherings. In keeping with the simplicity of the surroundings, freshly prepared spring rolls are served because they can be eaten without the fuss of utensils. The hot pink gerberas, placed in a teak container which also doubles as an ice bucket, add a touch of exuberance to the occasion.

left A 19th-century Ming-style bamboo jacket graces the wall and a Burmese lion coconut-husker watches over a tray of spring rolls. The iron balls from India were originally used to hold oil lamps; lighting the way of elephant keepers as they guided their herds at night.

page 55 Individual yellow roses in glass pebble vases rest like dew drops on the Keyaki wood table. Now a stunning feature of the living room, the table is in fact an old Japanese warehouse door, complete with original large doorlock hardware and wheels.

above The serene expression of the beautifully carved angel from Thailand casts a spell of tranquility over the room. White orchids and a silk shawl are draped over a Chinese merchant's jar, once used to store pickled vegetables or eggs.

a touch of zen • asian appetizers

Irresistible spring rolls, a melange of subtle and exotic flavors, are served with a chili dipping sauce for a casual evening with friends. And the perfect cocktails to sip while enjoying the appetizers are refreshing soursop daquiries. The intriguingly named soursop, also known as guanabana, is a prickly, kidney-shaped fruit; its flavor is somewhere between that of mango and a pineapple. The Chinese classify soursop as a "cooling" fruit and it makes an ideal drink with which to quench your thirst on a hot, sticky summer day.

spring rolls

ingredients
filling
2 teaspoons vegetable oil
2 cloves garlic, minced
1 tablespoon finely chopped fresh ginger
1/2 pound lean ground pork
1/2 cup finely chopped scallions
1 cup canned water chestnuts, drained and chopped
1/2 cup crabmeat, fresh or canned, drain if using canned
2 tablespoons finely chopped cilantro leaves
2 tablespoons Chinese oyster sauce
1 tablespoon Thai fish sauce (nam pla)
Freshly ground black pepper to taste

25–30 (10 x 10-inch) sheets of spring roll wrappers, choose ones that do not contain egg
Vegetable oil for frying

To make the filling:
Heat vegetable oil in large skillet and add garlic and ginger, stirring until fragrant, about 30 seconds. Add pork and stir, breaking up meat into small bits. Cook until done or when pork loses its pinkness, about 3 to 5 minutes. Add scallions and cook for 1 minute. Remove skillet from heat and add water chestnuts, crabmeat, and cilantro to pork mixture. Mix oyster and fish sauces together and add to pork mixture. Add black pepper to taste and mix all ingredients until well incorporated.

To make the spring rolls:
Lay a sheet of wrapper diagonally on your working surface, with one of the corners facing you. Place a heaping tablespoon of filling horizontally across the lower third of the wrapper. Fold the corner closest to you over the filling towards the center. Roll once, gently but tightly, away from you. Fold the right corner over the center followed by the left and continue rolling away from you to completely enclose the filling. Moisten the last corner with water to seal. Let stand corner-side down.

To fry:
Pour vegetable oil into a heavy skillet to a depth of 1 inch. Set over medium heat until sizzling hot. Dip a wooden spoon in the hot oil; the oil should bubble and sizzle gently around the spoon when it is hot enough. Carefully place 4 to 5 spring rolls into the hot oil, taking care not to splatter the oil. Fry, turning several times until crisp and golden, about 5 minutes. Drain on paper towels. Let oil return to original frying temperature before adding a new batch of rolls to fry. Keep rolls warm by transferring them to a warm oven.
  Serve warm with Chili Sauce, recipe on page 33.
Makes about 25 rolls, serves 6.

presentation: *Wrap each roll in a Bibb or Boston lettuce leaf and tie together with the green portion of a blanched scallion. To blanch, dip scallions, trimmed of their white bulb end, into a pot of boiling water for about 15 seconds. Remove and plunge into a bowl of iced water to refresh; this stops the cooking process and sets the color. Pat dry with a paper towel. Blanching softens the scallions so they can be tied around the rolls and knotted without breaking.*

Spring Rolls.

soursop daiquiries

ingredients
½ a soursop or 4 fresh mangos
⅛ cup lime juice
2½ cups crushed ice
Sugar syrup to taste
½ cup rum (optional)
½ cup Cointreau (optional)

For a fruit cocktail:
Peel the skin and remove the seeds from the fruit. Put the flesh into a blender or juice extractor with the lime juice, crushed ice and a little sugar syrup. Blend until smooth. Pour into glasses and serve.

For daiquiries:
Add rum and the Cointreau to the fruit cocktail above and blend a second time. Pour into glasses and serve. For mango daiquiries, simply substitute 4 mangoes for the soursop. Experiment with a wide variety of fresh tropical fruit such as kiwi fruit, watermelon, and papaya for non-alcoholic and alcoholic daiquiries.
Serves 4.
presentation: *Decorate glasses with slices of star fruit or dragon fruit.*

the pool house

sushi and cocktails

the pool house

left *A unique living room: rest and relax or splash and swim. The narrow but long pool takes full advantage of the depth of the traditional shophouse.*

page 65 *This dramatic floral display is a good example of keeping it simple: agapanthus, a few sprays of wild orchid and a large leaf from the elephant ear plant—just add water.*

Water, water everywhere . . . A living room may not be the usual location for a swimming pool, but that is the delightful surprise that awaits you upon entering this unconventional but stunning home.

The occupants insisted on having an indoor pool, and the living room was the only possible location, given the typically deep and narrow structure of this renovated shophouse. In keeping with the clean lines of the room and the serenity of the water, simple furnishings were chosen to create an informal yet elegant oasis where it is possible to both entertain and cool off in the pool. The fabrics chosen for the cushions and furniture are strong and bright, adding warmth and color to an interior that is otherwise cool and minimal. The high ceilings and stark white walls are emphasized by the length of the graceful tropical plants that stretch their way up to the light.

Poolside entertaining, especially the outside sort, is a wonderful way to celebrate on hot summer evenings (or any evening if you live in the tropics). The pool itself offered a unique design opportunity for entertaining. Rather than trying to play down its presence, we decided to dress it up and turn it into a shimmering indoor lake. For a more structured floral arrangement than flowers floating on the water, we placed wild orchid and agapanthas on bamboo poles and stretched them across the water; the vivid yellow and purple hues of the flowers contrasting beautifully with the turquoise water. (This arrangement is also easy to remove for guests who want to swim.)

For a relaxed evening gathering of friends, we planned a menu that is both casual and stylish, and perhaps just a little unconventional: like the house itself. Sushi—simple yet always refined —is served with iced sake as cool and transparent as the water itself.

far left *A frozen sake bottle decorated with wild orchids. You can present all sorts of drinks in decorative frozen containers. See page 123.*
left *Platters of azure blue glass that evoke the sea are the perfect platters on which to serve sushi, the food of the sea. When serving Japanese food, try using crockery that contrasts in shape with the food you are serving.*

the pool house . **sushi and cocktails**

The hard-to-beat sophistication yet sheer simplicity of sushi was the inspiration for this menu. The easy to prepare dishes include fresh salmon with a sesame-soy dressing, pickled daikon maki, and cherry tomatoes stuffed with crabmeat. The important thing to remember when preparing raw fish is to buy impeccably fresh sashimi-quality fish from a reputable fish market and to have them pack it with dry ice to ensure its freshness on the ride home.

daikon maki

ingredients

3 sheets of toasted nori, cut in half lengthwise or parallel to the lines on the seaweed

2 1/2 cups sushi rice (see recipe on the opposite page)

1 long piece takuan or pickled daikon radish, sliced lengthwise into 6 strips, each 1/2-inch wide

You will need a sushi mat made of strips of bamboo to shape the rolls. They are inexpensive and can be found in Japanese or other Asian markets.

Place the mat flat on your working surface. Place 1 sheet of the nori horizontally on the mat. The length of one end of the nori should be lined up with the bottom of the mat. Moisten your hands and spread a small handful of rice evenly over the nori, leaving an approximately 1/4-inch band at the far end. Center a daikon strip horizontally across the sushi rice. Holding the daikon in place, lift the end of the mat closest to you and roll the nori over the daikon to meet the rice on the side farthest away. Adjust the roll into a teardrop shape by pinching the ends which meet tightly together.

Remove the mat and cut the roll in half crosswise. Then cut each half into thirds leaving you with 6 pieces. Repeat the process with the remaining sheets of nori and ingredients. Makes 36 pieces.

notes: Nori *are the thin sheets of dried seaweed commonly used in Japanese and Korean cuisine. They are sold in stacks of several sheets either toasted or untoasted. They can be found in Japanese and Korean grocery stores.*

Takuan is a daikon radish which has been pickled. It is yellow in color and has a sweet-sour flavor with a slight crunch. Sliced takuan *is served as an accompaniment with Japanese meals. It is sold by the half piece in the refrigerated section of Japanese markets.*

Experiment with various fillings using the nori *and sushi rice: strips of omelet, pieces of avocado, etc.*

Salmon Tartare (middle) and Daikon Maki (bottom).

sushi rice

ingredients

1 cup Japanese rice
2 cups water
2 tablespoons vinegar
1/2 tablespoon sugar
1 teaspoon salt

Rinse rice until water runs clear. Drain well and transfer to a saucepan. Add water and soak rice for 20 minutes. Bring to a boil, then reduce to a simmer, cover and cook for 20 minutes. Remove from heat and let sit for 20 minutes covered.

Mix together the vinegar, sugar and salt until the sugar has dissolved.

Transfer the cooked rice to a wide, nonreactive bowl and spread the rice evenly around the bottom and the sides. Sprinkle the vinegar mixture evenly over the rice, taking care not to add too much liquid (you may not need all of the vinegar mixture). Gently mix the rice with a large wooden spoon until vinegar mixture is well absorbed. Cover rice with a damp tea towel and let cool.

note: *Sushi rice can be made a day in advance and stored in the refrigerator, covered tightly with plastic wrap. Let the rice come to room temperature before using.*

the pool house . **sushi and cocktails**

sesame style salmon tartare

ingredients

3/4 pound fresh sashimi-quality salmon, skinned and boned
1 cup peeled, seeded and diced cucumber
2 tablespoons finely sliced scallions
1 tablespoon chopped cilantro leaves
2 tablespoons roasted pine nuts, finely chopped
1/4 cup sesame dressing
30 shiso leaves

sesame dressing

1 tablespoon sesame paste
4 teaspoons light soy sauce
1 tablespoon rice wine vinegar
1 tablespoon finely diced ginger
2 cloves garlic, finely diced
1 tablespoon fine sugar
1/4 cup sesame oil

For the salmon:
Cut the salmon into 1/4-inch square pieces. Combine salmon, cucumber, scallions, cilantro leaves, pine nuts and sesame dressing (see below) in a bowl and toss until well mixed. *Makes about 30 hors d'oeuvres-size servings.*

For the sesame dressing:
Whisk together sesame paste and soy sauce in a bowl. Whisk in vinegar. While stirring, add ginger, garlic, and sugar, and stir until sugar has dissolved. Whisk in sesame oil. Let dressing stand for at least 30 minutes to allow the flavors to blend together.

presentation: *Place a tablespoon of salmon mixture on a shiso leaf or a lettuce leaf.*

note: *Shiso leaves, aromatic with a subtle minty taste, make a refreshing contrast to the richness of the salmon. They are a popular garnish on Japanese dishes and can be found in Japanese markets.*

cherry tomatoes stuffed with crabmeat

ingredients

30 cherry tomatoes, choose large ones
4 ounces crabmeat, fresh or canned, drain if using canned
1 tablespoon finely diced shallot
2 tablespoons cream cheese
Pinch of salt, to taste
30 avocado slices
Flying fish roe or caviar of your choice

Slightly trim the bottom of the tomatoes so they can stand. Cut the tops of the tomatoes and gently scoop out the seeds and flesh.

Mix the crabmeat, diced shallot, cream cheese, and salt together until all ingredients are well combined.

Stuff each tomato with some crabmeat mixture, top with a slice of avocado and some flying fish roe or caviar.
Makes 30.

preparation: *Use a 1/4-inch diameter melon baller to hollow out cherry tomatoes. The tomatoes can be prepared and stuffed the day before. Top with avocado and roe just before serving as avocado flesh darkens when exposed to air. To prevent discoloration, sprinkle some lemon juice or vinegar on the exposed flesh.*

Cherry Tomatoes and Gari.

pickled ginger (gari)

ingredients

8 ounces young ginger
6 tablespoons rice vinegar
2 tablespoons mirin
2 tablespoons sake
5 teaspoons sugar

Brush the ginger under running water, then blanch in boiling water for 1 minute. Drain.

Put the vinegar, *mirin*, *sake* and sugar in a small saucepan and bring to a boil, stirring until the sugar dissolves. Allow to cool.

Put the ginger in a sterilized jar and pour the cooled vinegar over it. Cover and let ginger rest for 3–4 days before using. This will keep refrigerated for up to 1 month.

notes: *Pickled ginger, which will develop a pale pink color as it ages, is sliced and served with sushi. It can also be bought bottled from Asian grocery stores.*

Mirin is a rice wine used only for cooking; if it is not available, use 1 teaspoon of sugar as a substitute for one teaspoon of mirin. *Mirin is sold in bottles and can be bought from Asian grocery stores.*

java style

an indonesian buffet

left *The living room, decorated with Chinese and Javanese furniture, provides the backdrop to a sumptuous platter of Indonesian finger food.*

Open courtyards where the rain cascades down and an open kitchen are just two of the features that make this house so interesting. Rich wooden cabinets and other furnishings from East Java fit this open breezy space to a tee. The beauty of this furniture is such that you need only a few key pieces to decorate a room; the strong lines and warm patina of the finishes add drama to any setting. As the spaces are large and open, the furniture is used to define the living areas. Because of their size and durability, Javanese cabinets and furnishings are ideal for storage or entertainment centers, as well as looking fabulous on their own. Javanese furniture can be happily blended with interiors that are more Western than this tropical home; although, you will probably find that once you've added a few pieces, you'll want to continue with the Indonesian theme and add samples of the many wonderful fabrics, furnishings and sculptures that can be found all over the archipelago.

The style and spices of the South Seas blow freely through this home. In keeping with the unhindered flow of the living spaces, the entertaining style here tends to be both casual and progressive. We started with hors d'oeuvres in the kitchen and moved to the next room for a delicious buffet that samples the fragrant and fiery delights of Indonesian cuisine. The partially open kitchen is an inviting and informal space in which the guests gather to gossip, drink apéritifs, and keep the cook company while the evening's buffet dinner is prepared: a succulent array of satays, salsa and seafood. *Jodags*, the wooden lanterns from Java, are filled with candles; in the days before electricity, *jodags* were filled with oil and lit. Used here as rustic candleholders, they cast a flickering light over freshly cut coconut and flaming chilies.

These are the simple pleasures of life. Add a few banana leaves to the setting and you really could be in Java.

far left The quintessential elements of Indonesian cuisine—the spice box and the coconut. Behind them are traditional Indonesian oil lamps or jodags.

top left The courtyard is an integral feature of the shophouse. Not only is it an ideal area in which to entertain, but encourages much needed evening breezes to flow through the house.

below left Hand-carved wooden tools are displayed on a long wooden chest that adds warmth and interest to an otherwise dull space beneath the stairs.

java style. an indonesian buffet

This buffet contains a mouth-tingling array of textures and flavors from the Indonesian archipelago. Chicken and mushroom satays, succulent roasted squid, and cilantro crab cakes are served with peanut and chili sauces, while a sweet-sour pineapple and cucumber salsa offers a crunchy contrast. Although not Indonesian, we've added tortillas to the platter, providing you with the option of making your own rolls. The mild taste of the tortillas is a nice foil for the spicy flavors of the Indonesian food. Tortillas can be bought either fresh or frozen from your local supermarket. To heat, loosely wrap a stack of tortillas in aluminum foil and place in a warm oven for about 5 minutes. If you are using the frozen ones, allow them to defrost first.

cilantro crab cakes

ingredients

2 tablespoons diced shallot
3/4 cup cooked crabmeat (if using canned, drain thoroughly)
1/2 cup bread crumbs
2 tablespoons chopped cilantro leaves
2 eggs, lightly beaten
1 teaspoon Worcestershire sauce
Several drops Tabasco, to taste
Salt to taste

Combine the shallot, crabmeat, bread crumbs, and cilantro in a bowl. Mix the eggs, Worcestershire sauce, Tabasco and salt together in a small bowl. Stir the egg mixture into the crab and bread crumb mixture until everything is well combined, taking care not to break up the lumps of crabmeat. Form crab cakes into flattened rounds, each about $2^{1}/_{2}$ inches wide and $1/2$ inch thick, and place on baking sheet. The crab cakes can be covered in plastic wrap and refrigerated for up to 4 hours at this point. When ready to cook, place the cakes in a preheated oven at 350 ° F and bake until golden brown, about 15 to 20 minutes.

Makes about 10 cakes.

presentation: *Serve all the dishes for this buffet together on a large platter covered with banana leaves. Freshly cut banana leaves make excellent natural serving platters and can also be used as placemats. Look for them at your local vegetable stand or in Asian markets.*

chicken satay

ingredients
marinade

2 cloves garlic, roughly chopped
2 onions, chopped
1 teaspoon curry powder
1 teaspoon ground cumin
1 teaspoon ground ginger
2 stalks lemongrass, chopped
(see preparation notes beneath satay sauce recipe)

1 pound chicken fillets

Place marinade ingredients in a small food processor and blend. Remove from the processor and add the chicken to the marinade. Marinate for 30 minutes.

Thread the chicken on skewers and cook on a hot grill.

Serve immediately with satay sauce.

Makes 10 skewers.

preparation: *If you are using wooden skewers for the satays, always soak them in water for several hours before placing them on the grill, to prevent burning.*

Chicken Satay (left), Satay Sauce (top) and Chili Sauce (bottom).

satay sauce

ingredients
2 tablespoons vegetable oil
12 shallots, finely chopped
1 1/2 teaspoons dried shrimp paste (blachan)
1 teaspoon cayenne
2 stalks lemongrass, finely chopped (see notes)
1 can coconut milk (10 fluid ounces)
2 tablespoons sugar
2 tablespoons chunky peanut butter
1 teaspoon salt
2 tablespoons chopped cilantro leaves

Heat the oil in a skillet and cook the shallots, shrimp paste, cayenne and lemongrass until fragrant, about 5 minutes.

Add the coconut milk, sugar, peanut butter and salt and cook, stirring constantly for about 10 to 15 minutes.

Remove from heat and stir in the cilantro leaves.
Makes about 1 cup.

preparation: *Lemongrass is a slim bulb with a lemony scent and flavor. To use, peel off the tough outer layers, cut away the top two-thirds of the stalk and trim the root end. Use the remaining third of the lower, tender portion of the bulb. Lemongrass needs to be finely chopped or pounded to release its fragrance.*

java style . an indonesian buffet

mushroom satay

ingredients

marinade
2 cloves garlic, minced
1 teaspoon fresh grated ginger
2 tablespoons cilantro leaves, chopped
3 tablespoons fish sauce (nam pla)
2 tablespoons sesame oil

20 shiitake mushrooms, stems removed

For the marinade:
Combine the garlic, ginger and cilantro leaves. Whisk fish sauce and sesame oil together in a small bowl and add to the garlic, ginger and cilantro mixture. Stir well.

Add the mushrooms to the marinade and coat well. Marinate for 1 hour.

Thread 2 mushrooms onto each skewer and cook on a hot grill.
Makes 10 skewers.

pineapple & cucumber salsa

ingredients
1 cup pineapple, sliced into small, thin pieces
1 cup Japanese cucumber, peeled and sliced into small, thin pieces
1/4 cup diced red onion (optional)
2 tablespoons rice vinegar
1 tablespoon sugar
1 small chili pepper, or more to taste, finely chopped

In a bowl, combine pineapple and cucumber pieces, and the onion if using.

In a small bowl, stir together vinegar, sugar and chili until sugar is dissolved.

Add vinegar mixture to pineapple-cucumber mixture and toss well.

Before serving, let salsa stand for 30 minutes at room temperature or up to 4 hours, refrigerated and covered with plastic wrap.
Makes 2 cups.

Main dish: Roasted Squid.

roasted squid

ingredients

2 tablespoons extra-virgin olive oil
4 cloves garlic, chopped
Salt and ground black pepper, to taste
1 pound squid, cleaned and cut in half lengthwise
2 tablespoons chopped cilantro leaves

Mix the oil, garlic and salt and pepper together in a small bowl. Add squid to oil mixture and toss until well coated.

Place the seasoned squid in a baking dish and roast in a preheated 450 ° F oven until squid is cooked but still tender, about 10 to 15 minutes.

To serve, slice squid into bite-sized pieces and toss with cilantro leaves.
Serves 10 as a side dish.

asian accents
curried flavors

asian accents

This home is a perfect example of Occident meets Orient. The occupants of the house returned to live in Asia for the second time and knew exactly what to bring with them. In fact, the table from the restaurant where the husband proposed has followed them everywhere, and has a place of prominence in their foyer. It is no surprise therefore that anniversaries are a cause for celebration in this home. Special occasions such as birthdays and anniversaries are a great excuse to host a intimate dinner with those special people in your life.

The celebrations begin at the bar overlooking the enclosed courtyard. Get the evening off to a tasty start with pappadums and raita. A celebration means fun and to put people in the right mood, the dining table has been set with special sparkle and decorated with silver table accessories and silver placemats. Antique Cambodian and Thai silver boxes are filled with pink roses, and silver beads and ribbons are wrapped around napkins. Don't be afraid to be creative, this table is a festive cornucopia of styles and colors. Cross cultural boundaries with your decor: Here we've mixed Cambodian and Thai silver boxes with modern frosted glass plates. Metallic pens, which are readily available from stationary stores, have been used to decorate the name cards. The custom-made "lazy suzan" has been decorated with tulips and roses. Just before guests arrive, fragrant rose petals are scattered on the table like confetti. A round table makes conversation easy and you don't have to worry about whom you seat at the head. The lights have been dimmed and two Lozal dolls, handmade by Tibetan monks, observe the festivities. A lavish Indian meal awaits the guests.

asian accents . curried flavors

Since we are celebrating, dinner is rich, decadent and inspired by India. Light, crispy pappadums are served with a cooling raita with the pre-dinner drinks. A starter is not necessary because of the richness of the main course, a creamy yet spicy chicken curry served with the finest basmati rice and accompanied by a mild okra dish. To finish a special evening, a meltingly smooth but rich Indian ice cream is served for dessert—with champagne, of course.

raita & pappadums

ingredients
2 small cucumbers, peeled, seeded and finely chopped
Salt
2 cups plain yogurt
1 teaspoon ground cumin
Pappadums

Put cucumber into a sieve and sprinkle with salt. Leave for $1/2$ hour to drain excess water.
   Beat yogurt with a fork until smooth. Mix cucumber and remaining ingredients into yogurt and transfer to a serving bowl.
   Serve with pappadums.
Makes 2 cups.

note: You can buy pappadums by the box at your local Indian grocer.

creamy cardamom chicken

ingredients
3 cups plain yogurt
1 tablespoon ground cardamom
4 whole chicken breasts, boned and skinned

3 tablespoons vindaloo paste
$3^{1}/2$ tablespoons unsalted butter
$3^{1}/2$ tablespoons flour
1 cup chicken broth
2 cups cream
$3/4$ cup tomato paste (one 6-ounce can)
1 tablespoon garam masala
1 tablespoon cayenne (optional)

Combine the yogurt and cardamom in a bowl and add the chicken. Cover with plastic wrap and refrigerate for 6 hours. Preheat oven to 350 ° F. Remove chicken from refrigerator and let it warm to room temperature. Remove chicken from marinade, shaking off as much of the marinade as possible. Place chicken pieces in a single layer on a baking sheet and bake in oven until cooked through, about 25 to 30 minutes. Let cool.
   Cook the *vindaloo* paste in a large pot over high heat, stirring constantly for about 2 minutes to release the flavors. Lower the heat and whisk in butter and flour and cook for about 2 minutes. Add chicken broth and continue whisking until the mixture becomes thick, about 3 minutes. Mix in the cream, tomato paste and *garam masala* over a low heat and cook for about 3 minutes.
   Cut the cooled chicken into bite-sized pieces and add to sauce and heat for 2 minutes. Add the cayenne if you like things hot. Remove from heat and serve over basmati rice.
Serves 6–8.

okra with mustard seeds

ingredients
3 tablespoons ghee or vegetable oil
1 tablespoon whole black mustard seeds
1 large onion, diced
$1/2$ teaspoon ground turmeric
$1/2$ teaspoon cayenne
$1^{1}/4$ pounds okra, trimmed (if okra are large, cut in half or thirds)
$1/2$ cup water

Heat oil or ghee over high heat in a large skillet. When oil is hot, add the mustard seeds and immediately cover with lid to contain the seeds, which will pop. This should take a few seconds. After the seeds have popped, add onion and cook until soft.
   Add turmeric, cayenne, okra, and water. Stir well, reduce heat, cover and cook until okra is tender but not overcooked, about 7 minutes.
Serves 6-8.

Creamy Cardamom Chicken.

indian ice cream

ingredients

4 quarts whole milk
1 cup sugar
2-4 tablespoons skinned pistachio nuts, chopped
4 tablespoons almond, finely ground (optional)

falooda

3 cups cornstarch
8 cups water

Put the milk into a wide, heavy pan and cook over very low heat. Stir constantly until the milk is reduced to about 4 cups and becomes a caramel color. Stir the sides of the pan constantly to prevent the milk from scalding. Add the sugar and nuts, and allow to cool. Freeze in individual metal containers such as jelly molds. Unmold and serve with *falooda*.

To make the *falooda*:
Dissolve the cornstarch in 2 cups of water. Heat the remaining water in a pan, add the blended cornstarch and cook to make a thick jell. While the mixture is still hot, put into a press capable of making fine threads the size of vermicelli. Fill a bowl full of cold water right up to the brim and set the press over the water so that when the falooda is pushed through the press, it immediately touches the water. Push all the jell through the press. Store in water until required and drain to serve.
Serves 8.

presentation: *Place 3 squares of ice cream on a plate and arrange some* falooda *in the middle.*

ethnic chic
cajun to asian

ethnic chic

left *The large hand-painted screen adds a striking bolt of color to the room and breaks up the large space, creating an intimate corner for conversation.*

below right *A mass of dried willow branches fans out from the tall woven basket used as a vase; the sharp twisted forms contrast with the smooth simple shapes of the bowls displayed on top of the wooden cabinet.*

The rich, sumptuous colors and textures of Africa and the Orient come together in a celebration of styles in this exotically furnished home.

Deep earth tones and ocher yellows weave their way through the batiks of Indonesia and dance across the primitive paintings that decorate the walls. Handcarved furnishings made from rare wood sit like sculptures amid the flickering light of the candles. Freshly cut giant heliconia and ginger, exotic tropical flowers brought in from nearby Malaysia, scent the warm night air and add a touch of mystery to the evening's atmosphere.

Natural materials have been used to furnish and decorate this room; the dining table centerpiece of yellow orchids seems to sprout naturally from a sculpted iron boat, setting the scene for a casual but chic dinner with friends.

ethnic chic

left Each place setting is highlighted with flowers in tiny vases that have been individually wrapped in batik. Asia has a wide variety of beautiful handmade fabrics which can be incorporated into your decorating schemes.

below The rather severe and formal beauty of the teak and cane settee from East Java is softened with the addition of warm and comfortable cushions. Marinated olives and slices of daikon combine for simple but flavorsome hors d'oeuvres.

ethnic chic . cajun to asian

Drawing on the exotic yet urbane appeal of the interior, a chic sit-down dinner has been created that starts in Asia, goes to New Orleans, and then back to Asia for a refreshing dessert. Light hors d'oeuvres of marinated olives and Japanese daikon slices are served with drinks before dinner, the marinated olives can be bought from your local deli. A spicy gumbo for the main course adds a Cajun touch and is hearty enough to require only rice with it. A luscious lychee mousse completes the meal.

cajun shrimp gumbo

ingredients

3 tablespoons olive oil
2 medium-sized onions, peeled and diced
2 cloves garlic, peeled and chopped finely
1 red bell pepper, peeled, seeds and membranes removed
1 (8-ounce) can peeled tomatoes
2 pounds shrimp, shells, tails and heads removed
4 cups okra, trimmed and chopped
1/2 teaspoon cayenne or to taste
1 teaspoon dried oregano
1/2 cup white wine
1 cup chicken stock
Salt and freshly ground black pepper

In a large skillet, heat the olive oil and cook onions and garlic over high heat until onions are wilted, about 3 minutes. Take care not to burn the garlic.

Add the bell peppers, tomatoes, shrimp, okra, cayenne, and oregano and cook for about 3 minutes, stirring frequently. Gently rub the oregano between your palms to release the flavor before adding it.

Add white wine and continue to stir, scraping the bottom of pan. Cook for about 3 minutes. Add chicken stock, reduce heat to a simmer and cover. Simmer for 5 minutes. Salt and pepper to taste. Serve with onion rice.

Serves 6.

presentation: To serve, place a mound of rice in the center of the plate and spoon the gumbo around it.

onion rice

ingredients

4 tablespoons olive oil
2 medium onions, diced
3 cups rice
6 cups water
Worcestershire sauce, to taste
Salt

Heat a saucepan and add the oil. Add the onions and cook until lightly browned. Add the rice and stir, coating it with the oil. Add water, the Worcestershire sauce, and salt to taste. Reduce heat to a simmer, cover and cook until the rice is cooked and the water absorbed.

Serves 6.

preparation: To dice onions, peel and cut the onion in half lengthwise. Trim the top end of the onion but keep the root end intact, it will help to hold the onion together. Place one half of the onion down on the cutting board and make a series of horizontal cuts, parallel to the cutting board, from the top to almost the root end but do not cut through the root. Then make a series of vertical slices, again taking care not to cut the root. Hold the onion firmly and cut crosswise into dice. Discard the root end that is left.

Cajun Shrimp Gumbo.

lychee mousse with sweet raspberry sauce

ingredients

3 tablespoons water
4 teaspoons plain gelatin powder
2 cups lychee purée (see below)
1 1/4 cups heavy cream or whipping cream

lychee purée

3 cups fresh or canned lychees
2–3 tablespoons confectioners' sugar, more or less to taste

sweet raspberry sauce

3 cups fresh or frozen raspberries
2–3 tablespoons sugar, or more to taste
Juice of 1/2 lemon
Makes about 1/2 cup sauce

Place water in saucepan and sprinkle in gelatin. Gently heat water and stir until gelatin has dissolved. Don't let the water boil. Remove from heat and let cool to lukewarm. Stir in lychee purée and let stand until mixture begins to thicken, about 20 minutes.

Whip cream with an electric mixer until medium peaks form. Stir 2 tablespoons of whipped cream into lychee purée, then fold in remaining whipped cream. Fill molds with mousse and gently tap the bottom against table top to eliminate air bubbles. Chill for at least 4 hours before unmolding.

For lychee purée: If using fresh lychees, peel and cut flesh away from pit. Purée in blender, adding powdered sugar to taste. For canned lychees, drain, omit sugar and blend.

For the sauce: Combine all ingredients in a saucepan and bring to a boil. Reduce heat and simmer until thickened, about 10 minutes. Remove from heat and push sauce through a fine sieve with a spatula to remove seeds. Let cool and transfer to squeeze bottle.

Makes about 3 1/2 cups of mousse or 8 individual (3 fluid-ounce) molds.

presentation: *To serve, unmold mousse onto plate and squeeze raspberry sauce circles around mousse.*

a moonlit courtyard

twilight supper

a moonlit courtyard

left *Welcome your guests by hanging Chinese lanterns from the trees outside your house. Or place candles in mini terra-cotta cups to lead the way to the party (see page 124).*

Twilight is the perfect time to unwind with family and friends. When the heat of the day begins to wane and the first stars quietly emerge to decorate the evening sky, it's time to host an outdoor party and experience the end of the day and the beginning of night.

No longer is the barbecue an occasion where badly cooked food, hard seats and insect bites are an accepted part of the evening's offerings. When entertaining moved outdoors, the purveyors of lifestyle goods followed, and now functional and stylish outdoor furniture, cooking equipment and crockery are all readily available in an infinite variety of forms. So, you can now hold your alfresco events, whether they be casual or sophisticated, without sacrificing comfort or style. Dress up your surroundings with rustic curios or statues, and bring the comfort of your living room to your outdoor furniture with bright, tropical print cushions. Remember though, when you are entertaining outdoors, your garden should be the star attraction, not the furniture. Let the scents, colors, and patterns of nature enhance your outdoor entertaining area. Perfume the evening air with the scents of jasmine, frangipani or lilies potted in attractive terra-cotta pots. You can also use these to fill dull corners or to supplement your garden if it is not looking its best.

As night falls, you will need to light your party. Line your patio edges with rows of candles and let their flickering light perform shadow dances on the nearby walls. The magical quality of candlelight adds a touch of festivity to any occasion. The colorful translucent fish lanterns (featured on the following pages) are often carried by children during the Chinese August Moon festival. Placed in the center of a glass table and lit by candles, this school of lantern fish makes a whimsical and charming centerpiece.

Keep the menu simple but interesting. The days of sawdust sausages and limp coleslaw are fortunately behind us; today's outdoor cook presents food that is clean but flavorsome. A crispy salad with something marinated and grilled is ideal. You don't want to be rushing in and out of the house to check on what's cooking indoors. Summer fruits, abundant in flavor and variety, are a cool and easy way to finish the meal.

a moonlit courtyard

right Use colorful handmade tiles as an alternative to a tablecloth on your outdoor furniture. These beautiful Peranakan tiles were often used to decorate the facades of shophouses.
far right A great outdoor setting: the patterned furniture and festive fish lanterns are bright, welcoming and casual.

left Translucent fish lanterns, often carried by children during the Chinese "Moon" festival in August. Use festive seasonal ornaments such as banners, candles or lanterns from different cultures to bring a fiesta feel to your entertaining.

above A Chinese lantern brings a glow to this corner of the courtyard. Look for these bright paper lanterns at stores in your local Chinatown.

a moonlit courtyard . twilight supper

Start your evening with fresh shrimp noodle rolls served with a tangy lime and fish sauce dressing; a good recipe to make in advance. If you feel like lingering over the appetizers, supplement the noodle rolls with spicy pork bundles: mouthfuls of spicy, seasoned pork topped with fresh herbs, served in a leaf of soft butter lettuce. Follow the rolls with grilled salmon, nutty wild rice, and a mixed green salad with calamansi lime dressing. To stay cool, serve a frosty tray of frozen grapes and mangosteen sorbets—a refreshing finale to a hot summer evening.

shrimp noodle rolls

ingredients

10 ounces cellophane noodles
40 shrimp, peeled and deveined, remove the heads but leave the tails on
1-2 cups mint leaves
1-2 heads Bibb or Boston lettuce leaves, with tough center ribs removed
20 scallions, green part only, blanched then refreshed in ice water

Soften noodles in hot water for 15 minutes. Drain and cut into 3-inch lengths.

Cook shrimp briefly in boiling water for approximately 3 minutes. Be careful not to overcook the shrimp as they will get tough very quickly. Drain and let cool.

To assemble: Place a small bundle of noodles in the bottom portion of each lettuce leaf and put 3-4 mint leaves on the noodles. Starting from the end closest to you, roll the lettuce away from you over the noodles, continue rolling until the noodles are completely covered. Make sure that some of the noodles and the mint protude from either side of the leaf. Place the roll seam side down. Place 2 shrimp on top of the roll and holding the shrimp and the roll together, wrap a length of scallion around the whole bundle and tie firmly, the tie should be at the top of the bundle.

Serve with the lime and fish sauce dressing from the Beef Salad on Cucumber Slices recipe on page 121. You may need to double the quantity of the dressing.
Makes 20 rolls.

spicy pork bundles

ingredients

1 tablespoon vegetable oil
2 cloves garlic, minced
2 tablespoons finely chopped fresh ginger
1 pound lean ground pork
2 teaspoons sesame oil
2 teaspoons soy sauce
1 teaspoon cayenne or chili oil, more to taste
4 tablespoons finely chopped cilantro leaves
2 tablespoons finely chopped mint leaves
1 tablespoon freshly squeezed lime juice
2 small red chilies, finely sliced
2 scallions, finely chopped
Hoisin sauce
1 to 2 heads of Bibb or Boston lettuce, leaves separated

Heat vegetable oil in a large skillet. Add garlic and ginger and stir until fragrant, about 30 seconds. Add pork and stir, breaking up meat into small bits, until done or when no longer pink, 3 to 5 minutes. Add scallions and cook for 1 minute.

Whisk sesame oil, soy sauce, and cayenne together and add to pork mixture. Stir to mix and cook for 1 minute. Remove from heat and stir in the cilantro, mint leaves and lime juice. Transfer to a serving bowl and garnish with fresh chilies and scallion.

Serve with whole lettuce leaves and hoisin sauce. Let guests help themselves by spooning some pork mixture on to a lettuce leaf and topping with a teaspoon of hoisin sauce.

note: Serve additional scallions, chili, cilantro and mint leaves in separate bowls on the side so guests can top their pork bundles with extra garnishes if desired.

Shrimp Noodle Rolls.

salad *with* lime dressing

ingredients
1 head red oak leaf lettuce
2 heads Bibb lettuce
15 cherry tomatoes, cut in half

calamansi lime dressing
1/4 cup fresh calamansi lime juice
2 tablespoons vegetable oil
2 tablespoons white vinegar
1 tablespoon water
1 tablespoon sugar, or more to taste
2 teaspoons minced shallot
1 clove garlic, minced
2 tablespoons chopped fresh dill, or
1 tablespoon dried dill

Wash and thoroughly dry the lettuce leaves. Tear leaves into bite-size pieces and place in a salad bowl, add the tomatoes and toss with some dressing until lightly and evenly coated.

For the dressing:
Whisk lime juice and vegetable oil together until well mixed. Whisk in remaining ingredients and continue whisking until the sugar has dissolved. Taste the dressing and add more sugar if it is too sour.
Serves 10-12 as an accompaniment to the salmon.

note: *Calamansi, a small citrus fruit native to the Philippines, is prized for its tart juice.*

a moonlit courtyard . **twilight supper**

grilled *balsamic* and soy salmon

ingredients
½ salmon, deboned
2 tablespoons extra-virgin olive oil

soy-balsamic sauce
⅓ cup extra-virgin olive oil
3 tablespoons balsamic vinegar
1 tablespoon soy sauce
2 tablespoons chopped parsley
1 teaspoon grated fresh ginger (optional)
Makes about ⅔ cup

Brush both sides of the salmon half with olive oil. Place fish in a special hinged fish rack brushed with olive oil to prevent the fish from sticking.

Grill salmon for 10 minutes per inch of thickness. Skin should be crispy and flesh fork-tender. Carefully place fish on a large platter and serve with soy-balsamic sauce.

For the sauce:
Whisk the olive oil and balsamic vinegar together until well blended. Add the soy sauce while continuing to whisk. Stir in parsley and ginger if using.
Serves 10-12.

note: *You can also cut the salmon into individual-sized fillets and roast in the oven. Lightly oil a baking sheet and place the fillets on it skin-side up. Roast in a 475 ° F oven for approximately 15 minutes.*

mangosteen sorbet

ingredients
⅔ cup water
⅔ cup sugar
2 cups mangosteen flesh (about 25 to 30 mangosteens or substitute with canned mangosteen)
3 tablespoons rum
1 teaspoon freshly squeezed lime juice
Pinch of salt

Bring water and sugar to a boil in a saucepan. Stir occasionally to dissolve the sugar and cook until a syrup forms, about 3 minutes. Remove from heat and let cool.

Purée mangosteen flesh in a food processor or blender. Transfer to a bowl and add sugar syrup, rum, lime juice and salt, and mix together.

Process mixture in ice cream maker according to manufacturer's directions. Or, if making by hand, transfer the mixture to a baking pan and freeze for 6 hours. Remove from freezer and blend in food processor or blender. Return mixture to freezer for at least 5 more hours or until ready to serve.
Serves 10.

presentation: *For a cool, frosty presentation that's perfect for a hot summer evening, serve sorbet in frozen mangosteen "bowls." Rinse and dry the empty mangosteen shells and the "lids." Place in the freezer until ready to serve. To serve, fill mangosteen shells with the sorbet, replace the lids and place on a serving platter. Or you can fill the shells and return them to the freezer until ready to serve. Serve with a bunch of frozen seedless grapes and cheese.*

notes: *The mangosteen fruit is native to Southeast Asia and has a thick, hard, eggplant-colored shell. The sweet, juicy white flesh is segmented and contains a pit. To remove the flesh, slice off the top quarter of the mangosteen and spoon out the flesh. Take a small paring knife and scrape the flesh away from the pit, taking care as the flesh is extremely slippery. Persimmons can be substituted for the mangosteens if desired.*

Mangosteen and Persimmon Sorbets.

wild rice

ingredients
10 cups chicken broth or water
2 tablespoons unsalted butter
1 teaspoon salt
5 cups wild rice

In a large pot, bring chicken broth or water, butter and salt to a boil. Add rice and bring to a second boil. Reduce heat and simmer, covered, for about 50 minutes, or until tender but firm to the bite. If all the liquid has not evaporated, drain rice in a sieve. Toss with additional butter if desired.
Serves 10-12.

note: *Taste your chicken broth. If it is already salted, you may want to omit the additional salt to the rice.*

indigo night

fabulous finger food

indigo night

Transform your home into a chic and sultry cocktail lounge. For a wonderfully grown-up party, blend the sophistication of a Manhattan cocktail lounge with the decadence of a scene from the Arabian Nights.

To create the mood, rivers of sheer, colored fabric were hung from the ceiling, the soft cascades of indigo, turquoise and pale green adding an air of fantasy to the occasion. Opulent jewel-toned cushions are scattered invitingly on the sofa for those who prefer quite and intimate conversation to the cocktail party chatter. The Arabian Nights ambience is conjured with colored-glass serving dishes and silver trays set on honeycombed wooden tabletops. Quintessential cocktail party elements were added to finish the lounge look: the martini glass, its cool, elegant shape an icon of 1950s chic (think Cary Grant); bar accessories such as cocktail shakers, swizzle sticks and olives; and cocktail napkins which are the perfect size for those irresistible mouthfuls of fabulous finger food.

This sophisticated look is not difficult to achieve but it does require a little preparation. The Arabian Nights mood was created by hanging layers of sheer fabric around the room curtain-style (see page 125). Once you've gathered your choice of fabric, the rest is easy and well worthwhile doing; the right decor can really make your party one to remember. Most of the finger foods served can be prepared well in advance and are a delicious mix of hot and spicy, and cool and refreshing flavors. Since we are going all out, hire a bartender to mix the drinks and help pass the hors d'oeuvres. This keeps the fun flowing and leaves you free to catch up with your friends; after all, the party is for you too.

indigo night . fabulous finger food

For a cocktail party, finger-food size hors d'oeuvres are a must so that your guests have one hand free to hold their drinks. The tangy shrimp dish below is the exception to this rule but it is so good we had to include it anyway. Most of the hors d'oeuvres presented here can be made at least partly in advance, which allows you to spend the maximum time with your guests and have as much fun as everyone else. The flavors here are truly international, from the ginger, cilantro and lime juice redolent of Asia to the sophisticated flavors of Europe.

dill & ginger shrimp starter

ingredients
1 pound shrimp, peeled and deveined
3 slices lemon

marinade
1/2 cup olive oil
2 tablespoons white wine vinegar
3 tablespoons Dijon mustard
1 clove garlic, minced
1 teaspoon or more grated fresh ginger
2 tablespoons chopped fresh dill
Cracked pepper
1/2 teaspoon sugar

Add shrimp and lemon to a pot of boiling water and boil for about 3 minutes or until shrimp is cooked. Take care not to overcook the shrimp or it will become tough. Drain shrimp thoroughly and let cool.

For the marinade:
Whisk together marinade ingredients. Add shrimp to marinade and mix together until shrimp is coated. Refrigerate until ready to serve.
Serves 8–10 as hors d'oeuvre-sized servings.

note: *This dish can be made one day ahead and also makes a wonderful starter. Simply place some marinated shrimp over mixed greens and serve as a salad course.*

parmesan stars

ingredients
1 1/2 cups Parmigiano-Reggiano cheese, finely grated
1 cup ricotta cheese
1 cup finely diced onion (slightly less than 1 large onion)
2 tablespoons cream
12 slices white bread, crusts removed

Preheat oven to 425 ° F.
Mix cheeses, onion and cream together. Spread 1 heaped tablespoon of the cheese mixture onto each slice of bread until the surface is evenly covered. Cut each slice into 4 triangular pieces and place on a baking sheet. Bake for 10–15 minutes or until golden brown and serve.
Makes about 48 mini toasts.

presentation: *For the festive presentation shown here, use a star-shaped cutter to cut out toasts. Spread cheese mixture onto bread, carefully cut out shapes with cutter and bake.*

preparation: *The cheese mixture can be made a day in advance and refrigerated.*

Fabulous Finger Food.

spiced nuts

ingredients
3/4 teaspoon cayenne
1/2 teaspoon curry powder
1/2 teaspoon salt
1/4 teaspoon ground coriander
1/4 teaspoon ground cinnamon
1/4 teaspoon ground ginger
2 tablespoons vegetable oil
2 cups shelled whole almonds or cashews

Preheat oven to 325 ° F.

Mix together all the dry ingredients except the nuts in a small bowl and set aside. Heat the oil in a skillet, preferably a nonstick one. Add the spice mixture and stir well. Cook until fragrant, about 1 minute. Place the nuts in a bowl, add the spice mixture, and toss well. Spread the nuts in a single layer on a baking sheet. Bake until fragrant, about 15 minutes. Remove the baking sheet from the oven and toss nuts with any spices and oil that have accumulated on the pan. Sprinkle with more salt if desired. Let nuts cool to room temperature.

Makes 2 cups.

note: *Nuts can be stored in an airtight container for up to a week.*

cheesy mushroom treats

ingredients
30 button mushrooms, stems removed
4 ounces brie cheese
1 small jar of sundried tomatoes packed in olive oil

Preheat oven to 425 ° F.

Cut brie into 30 pieces. Drain the sundried tomatoes and cut into 30 pieces.

Place mushroom caps upside down on a baking sheet. Stuff hollow part of the caps with brie and then sundried tomatoes. Place in the oven and bake until the cheese has melted, about 7 minutes As you transfer mushroom caps to the serving tray, gently blot the bottom on a paper towel to remove the liquid which has accumulated during baking. Makes 30.

note: *The mushroom caps can be stuffed, covered and refrigerated the night before. Just pop in hot oven to bake before serving.*

persian rolls

ingredients
3 (10 x 10-inch) frozen puff pastry sheets
9 gherkins
36 thin slices of sopressa salami, or any other salami of your choice

Preheat oven to 425 ° F.

Cut the pastry sheets in half. Cut each half into 3 even pieces lengthwise, resulting in 18 rectangles. Then make a diagonal cut across each rectangle. You should end up with 36 triangles.

Quarter gherkins lengthwise until you have about 36 quarters.

Place a triangle of puff pastry on your work surface with the wide end toward you. Place a slice of salami at the base end and top with a gherkin slice. Roll the wide end of the pastry around the salami and gherkin and continue rolling toward the point end. Place on a baking sheet with point-side down.

Bake until pastry is golden and puffed, 10 to 15 minutes.
Serves 6.

note: *The rolls can be made the day before and refrigerated. Bake before serving.*

Cheesy Mushroom Treats.

beef salad on cucumber slices

ingredients

dressing

2 tablespoons lime juice
1 tablespoon rice vinegar
1 tablespoon fish sauce (nam pla)
1 tablespoon sugar
2 bird's eye chilies, or more to taste, chopped
1/4 cup chopped mint leaves
1/4 cup chopped cilantro leaves

8 ounces very thinly sliced roast beef from the deli counter, torn into bite-size pieces
3 to 4 large cucumbers, peeled

For the dressing: whisk together lime juice, vinegar, fish sauce, sugar, and chilies in a bowl, until the sugar is dissolved. Toss beef with lime dressing and let stand for at least 15 minutes, or cover and refrigerate overnight. Just before serving, toss mint and cilantro with beef mixture.

Cut cucumbers crosswise into 1/2-inch-thick slices. Using a melon baller, scoop out a pocket from the center of each cucumber slice. Top each cucumber slice with a teaspoon of the beef mixture.

Makes about 30 slices.

presentation: *For a different presentation, use a cookie cutter to cut shapes from cucumber slices while discarding the peel at the same time. Choose a cutter which is just slightly smaller than the circumference of the cucumber slice. Cut cucumber into slices, then use cutter to cut shapes out of each slice.*

appendix

tips

in living color - stencil your napkins to fit the occasion

Finding the right napkins to match your setting can sometimes be a problem. An easy way around this is to make your own. All you need is cotton fabric or napkins, fabric paint, and a stencil of the pattern you wish to create. Take a damp kitchen sponge and dip into the paint. Blot the excess onto some newspaper. Place the stencil over the area to be decorated and dot it with the sponge until the coverage of color you desire has been achieved. Remove the stencil and let the paint dry completely before use. Your stenciling can be as simple or intricate as you want. If using different stenciling patterns or colors, make sure one design or color has dried completely before applying another. A great idea for cocktail napkins is to stencil your monogram.

form & feng shui - good fortune decor

Why not decorate with *feng shui*! Buy some *feng shui* bells and welcome prosperity and harmony into your home. Use sage sticks to purify new rooms and light prosperity candles. Clear the air and open the pathways to *chi'i* (energy) with *feng shui* peony and lemongrass-scented potpourri.

the comfort zone - versatile vegetables

Not only do pumpkins make excellent food containers, but they can be used as interesting flower containers as well. Other vegetables can be substituted for flowers to make interesting table arrangements and are an inexpensive and unusual alternative. Try using a whole, fresh cauliflower, green leaves still in place, as a centerpiece; or wrap fresh red chilies with raffia and make tiny bouquets. Fill a glass container with whole limes or lemons, tamarind pods or gourds.

tips . unique decorations and other fun ideas

pretty in pink - more quick tricks with puff pastry

Save leftover pastry trimmings to make mini *pain au chocolat*: Cut out small circles and fill with a piece of chocolate. Fold the ends together and press the edges firmly together. Bake at 375 ° F until golden. Or for mini apple turnovers, fill with applesauce and bake until golden—a great afternoon snack for the kids.

a touch of zen - the organic vase

Be creative in your choice of vase and use natural materials. The rustic appearance of this teak container/ice bucket is a perfect complement to the bright gerberas. Simply place a glass bowl inside the container and fill with water and your chosen blooms. Make orchids bloom from a woven Thai basket by inserting the stems into plastic florists tubes filled with water. These are available at most florists and allow you the flexibility of using a variety of unusual containers as vases, either upright or placed on their sides. The tubes are easily refilled and can be re-used numerous times.

the pool house - cool drinks for summer nights

Serve vodka, tequila or sake bottles in decorative ice containers. Use a milk carton, or any freezable container about 1 inch wider than your bottle and as tall. Place the bottle inside the container and fill with water to the neck of the bottle. Insert orchid stems, or whichever flower you prefer, into the water and freeze overnight. When frozen solid, peel away the carton. If using a nondisposable container, let stand for 15–30 minutes at room temperature until it can be easily removed. Place iced bottle back in freezer until ready to serve.

appendix

asian accents - the romantic table

To bring an extra sparkle to your table on special occasions, leave your more ordinary napkin holders in the cupboard and add a little romance in the form of these silver beads and ribbon which can be bought at most craft stores. Tie the ribbon in a bow around your folded napkin, then weave the beads in and out of the ribbon.

For the placecards, use fabric paint that comes in a squeeze bottle to make designs of your choice and color on blank business cards. The heavy fabric paint creates the attractive effect of raised lettering.

---

ethnic chic - exotically wrapped vases

As a change from the usual centerpiece, the flowers for this dinner were wrapped in batik and put in front of the individual place settings. Fill bud vases with water and then wrap in a 6-inch square piece of fabric that matches or complements your table linen; fasten by tying a smaller piece of fabric around the middle. Experiment with different patterns, making sure your fabric does not overwhelm your flowers.

---

a moonlit courtyard - the enchanted garden

An alternative to the Chinese lanterns we used (left) is to use mini terra-cotta pots as candleholders to illuminate your garden party. Hindus celebrate Deepavali, the festival of light, by filling small terra-cotta bowls with lamp oil. A thick wick is then placed into the oil for lighting. A row of these winding its way through your garden is a enchanting way to lead guests to the party. Take care not to leave an open flame unattended.

tips . unique decorations and other fun ideas

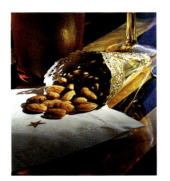

indigo night - lacy gold nut holders

The delicious spiced party nuts are even more appealing when served in these gold cones. To make the nut holders, gold doilies were shaped into cones and secured with scotch tape. If preferred, you could use stickers instead of tape. These pretty cones would also make ideal containers for candy at children's parties.

indigo night - bejeweled candles

Candlelight always adds ambience and to make the candles themselves look the part for our "cocktail chic meets Arabian Nights" theme, we dressed them in jeweled ribbons. Be sure to use the sort of candles that don't drip wax if you don't want to ruin your ribbons. For the star cocktail napkins in the picture above, a rubber stamp with a star design was dipped into gold fabric paint and stamped onto the center of the napkins.

indigo night - gossamer drapes

These curtains can be hung over windows, doorways or even over dull sections of wall that need a little color. First, buy lightweight fabric in your desired colors. For height, measure the height of your room and add 5 inches to the measurement, the width depends on where you plan to hang the curtains. Lay out each panel of fabric and overlap some of the panels. At one end of the fabric, bunch the material into gathers and use a strong safety pin (or several) to hold the gathers in place to make the curtains. Once all the gathers have been made, take strong hardware tape at least 1 inch wide and tape across the top of the curtain, making certain that a $1/2$ inch of the tape sticks out over the fabric. Using a ladder, stick your curtain to the desired space on your ceiling with the exposed part of the tape.

appendix

measurement and conversion tables

Measurements in this book are given in volume as far as possible. Teaspoon, tablespoon and cup measurements should be level, not heaped, unless otherwise indicated. Australian readers please note that the standard Australian measuring spoon is larger than the UK or American spoon by 5 ml, so use only 3/4 tablespoon when following the recipes.

liquid conversions

Imperial	Metric	US cups
1/2 fl oz	15 ml	1 tablespoon
1 fl oz	30 ml	1/8 cup
2 fl oz	60 ml	1/4 cup
4 fl oz	125 ml	1/2 cup
5 fl oz (1/4 pint)	150 ml	2/3 cup
6 fl oz	175 ml	3/4 cup
8 fl oz	250 ml	1 cup
12 fl oz	375 ml	1 1/2 cups
16 fl oz	500 ml	2 cups

Note:
 1 UK pint = 20 fl oz
 1 US pint = 16 fl oz

solid weight conversions

Imperial	Metric
1/2 oz	15 g
1 oz	30g
1 1/2 oz	50 g
2 oz	60 g
3 oz	90 g
3 1/2 oz	100 g
4 oz (1/4 lb)	125 g
5 oz	150 g
6 oz	185 g
7 oz	200 g
8 oz (1/2 lb)	250 g
9 oz	280 g
10 oz	300 g
16 oz (1 lb)	500 g (0.5 kg)
32 oz (2 lb)	1 kg

oven temperatures

Heat	Fahrenheit	Centigrade/Celsius	British Gas Mark
Very cool	225	110	1/4
Cool or slow	275–300	135–150	1–2
Moderate	350	175	4
Hot	425	220	7
Very hot	450	230	8

index

Index of recipes

appetizers
- Beef Salad on Cucumber Slices 121
- Cheesy Mushroom Treats 120
- Cherry Tomatoes Stuffed with Crabmeat 72
- Cilantro Crab Cakes 80
- Daikon Maki 70
- Dill and Ginger Shrimp Starter 118
- Easy Popiah 32
- Marinated Olives 98
- Mushroom Satay 82
- Parmesan Stars 118
- Persian Rolls 120
- Puff Pastry Canapés 53
- Roasted Squid 83
- Sesame Style Salmon Tartare 72
- Shrimp Noodle Rolls 108
- Smoked Salmon Ribbons 51
- Spicy Madeira Beef Puffs 52
- Spicy Pork Bundles 108
- Spring Rolls 62
- Vegetable Curry Puffs 50

beef
- Beef Salad on Cucumber Slices 121
- Beef Tenderloin 22
- Spicy Madeira Beef Puffs 52

bell peppers
- Cajun Shrimp Gumbo 98
- Caponata 22

bread
- Colonial Tuna Sandwiches 50
- Parmesan Stars 118

Cajun Shrimp Gumbo 98
Caponata 22

cheese
- Caper-Cream Cheese Spread 51
- Cheesy Mushroom Treats 120
- Cherry Tomatoes Stuffed with Crabmeat 72
- Ginger and Orange Cream 23
- Parmesan Stars 118

Cherry Tomatoes Stuffed with Crabmeat 72

chicken
- Chicken Rice 34
- Chicken Satay 80
- Creamy Cardamom Chicken 90

Chili Sauce 33
Chocolate Dipped Fruit 35

cilantro
- Cilantro Crab Cakes 80

Colonial Tuna Sandwiches 50

cream
- Green Tea Ice Cream 45

- Lychee Mousse with Sweet Raspberry Sauce 99
- Parmesan Stars 118
- Pumpkin Soup 42

Creamy Cardamom Chicken 90

cucumber
- Beef Salad on Cucumber Slices 121
- Pineapple and Cucumber Salsa 82
- Raita 90
- Smoked Salmon Ribbons 51

Daikon Maki 70
Daikon Slices 98

desserts
- Chocolate Dipped Fruit 35
- Fruit Salad with a Ginger and Orange Cream 23
- Green Tea Ice Cream 45
- Indian Ice Cream 91
- Lychee Mousse with Sweet Raspberry Sauce 99
- Mangosteen Sorbet 110

Dill and Ginger Shrimp Starter 118

Easy Popiah 32

eggplant
- Caponata 22

fish
- Grilled Balsamic and Soy Salmon 110
- Sesame Style Salmon Tartare 72
- Smoked Salmon Ribbons 51

fruit
- Chocolate Dipped Fruit 35
- Fruit Salad with Ginger and Orange Cream 23
- Lychee Mousse with Sweet Raspberry Sauce 99
- Mangosteen Sorbet 110
- Pineapple and Cucumber Salsa 82
- Pork Loin with Mango Salsa and Raspberry Sauce 44
- Soursop Daiquiries 63

Fruit Salad with a Ginger and Orange Cream 23

ginger
- Dill and Ginger Shrimp Starter 118
- Ginger and Orange Cream 23
- Pickled Ginger 73

Green Tea Ice Cream 45
Grilled Balsamic and Soy Salmon 110

Indian Ice Cream 91

Lychee Mousse with Sweet Raspberry Sauce 99

mango
- Pork Loin with Mango Salsa and Raspberry Sauce 44
- Soursop Daiquiries 63

Mangosteen Sorbet 110
Marinated Olives 98

appendix

mayonnaise
-Colonial Tuna Sandwiches   50
mushrooms
-Cheesy Mushroom Treats   120
-Mushroom Satay   82
-Sautéed Shiitake Mushrooms   44
-Spicy Madeira Beef Puffs   52
Mushroom Satay   82

noodles
-Shrimp Noodle Rolls   108

okra
-Cajun Shrimp Gumbo   98
-Okra with Mustard Seeds   90
olives
-Caponata   22
-Marinated Olives   98
Onion Rice   98

Pappadums   90
Parmesan Stars   118
pastry
-Persian Rolls   120
-Puff Pastry Canapés   53
-Spicy Madeira Beef Puffs   52
-Vegetable Curry Puffs   50
Pickled Ginger   73
Pineapple and Cucumber Salsa   82
pork
-Easy Popiah   32
-Pork Loin with Mango Salsa and Raspberry Sauce   44
-Spicy Pork Bundles   108
-Spring Rolls   62
Puff Pastry Canapés   53
Pumpkin Soup   42

Raita   90
rice
-Chicken Rice   34
-Daikon Maki   70
-Onion Rice   98
-Sushi Rice   71
-Wild Rice   111
Roasted Squid   83

salads   see vegetables
Salad with Lime Dressing   109
Satay Sauce   81
sauces, salsas, spreads, condiments and dressings
-Caper-Cream Cheese Spread   51
-Chili Sauce   33
-Ginger and Orange Cream   23
-Calamansi Lime Dressing   109
-Mango Salsa   44
-Pineapple and Cucumber Salsa   82
-Raita   90
-Raspberry Sauce   44
-Satay Sauce   81
-Sesame Dressing   72
-Soy Balsamic Sauce   110
-Sweet Raspberry Sauce   99
Sautéed Shiitake Mushrooms   44
seafood   see also fish
-Cajun Shrimp Gumbo   98
-Cherry Tomatoes Stuffed with Crabmeat   72
-Cilantro Crab Cakes   80
-Dill and Ginger Shrimp Starter   118
-Roasted Squid   83
-Shrimp Noodle Rolls   108
Sesame Style Salmon Tartare   72
shrimp
-Cajun Shrimp Gumbo   98
-Dill and Ginger Shrimp Starter   118
-Shrimp Noodle Rolls   108
Smoked Salmon Ribbons   51
soup
-Pumpkin Soup   42
Soursop Daiquiries   63
Spiced Nuts   119
Spicy Madeira Beef Puffs   52
Spring Rolls   62
Steamed Baby Kai-lan   43
Sushi Rice   71

tomatoes
-Cajun Shrimp Gumbo   98
-Caponata   22
-Cherry Tomatoes Stuffed with Crabmeat   72

vegetables, salads   see also individual vegetables
-Caponata   22
-Cheesy Mushroom Treats   120
-Mushroom Satay   82
-Okra with Mustard Seeds   90
-Pickled Ginger   73
-Pineapple and Cucumber Salsa   82
-Pumpkin Soup   42
-Salad with Lime Dressing   109
-Sautéed Shiitake Mushrooms   44
-Steamed Baby Kai-lan   43
-Vegetable Curry Puffs   50

Wild Rice   111
wine
-Cajun Shrimp Gumbo   98

yogurt
-Creamy Cardamom Chicken   90
-Raita   90